Paddy Maugg

From
Penguins *to* Paradise:
My Life as an Advertising Man

PADDY HAYES

authorHOUSE®

AuthorHouse™ UK
1663 Liberty Drive
Bloomington, IN 47403 USA
www.authorhouse.co.uk
Phone: UK TFN: 0800 0148641 (Toll Free inside the UK)
         UK Local: 02036 956322 (+44 20 3695 6322 from outside the UK)

Published by AuthorHouse 10/12/2020

ISBN: 978-1-6655-8067-0 (sc)
ISBN: 978-1-6655-8068-7 (hc)
ISBN: 978-1-6655-8066-3 (e)

Print information available on the last page.

This book is printed on acid-free paper.

Contents

Contents

Chapter 1

London, 1968–1972

"I know it's your first day," said Paul, my Account Director and mentor for the next couple of years, "but I want you to come with me to your first meeting with the 'Creatives'. Just remember that they are the ones who are meant to have all the smart ideas, not we 'Suits'. And it's your first day, so say nothing. Got it?"

I nodded, thinking that this job, my first in an advertising agency, was already feeling a bit strange – a whole new world.

"The situation is we're being threatened with losing the Penguin biscuit business if we can't come up with a new TV campaign idea," he continued. "So the Creatives are under a lot of pressure. We are going to review the progress they've made so far in finding something our client might be prepared to buy. But just remember, *schtum*!"

In the creative department we found a strange-looking bunch. In an open-necked shirt and grey suit, Sam, the Creative Director, looked the most 'civilised'. Jimmy, the Art Director, appeared to have difficulty looking any of us in the eye – not so much a shifty look, just someone who was totally lacking in confidence in a social setting. He sat picking small specks from his Levi's. Ed was the complete opposite – 'all mouth and trousers', as Paul later described him.

Unconventional as they were, this was the team that had created some of the agency's best campaigns.

"I'm sorry, Paul, but we're no further forward," Sam began. "There have been a couple of half ideas, but we've had to reject them all as unworkable."

To me, the long silence in the room went on for ages ... and ages. Uncomfortable with all the brooding around me, I ventured: "Have we ever thought of using real, live penguins? They look so cute."

"Shut up!" was Paul's immediate response.

Another long, long silence fell on the room as I squirmed in my seat.

"You know, there may be some mileage in that," said Sam after a while. "They say 'Never Work with Children or Animals', but penguins do look like absurd little men in dinner jackets. They certainly have the 'Aah!' factor. And no, we haven't thought about using them before. But it's only a creative execution idea you've just had. We still lack a creative platform, and a consumer promise, which together will make the customer want to buy. But just maybe this is a place to start ..."

A few moments later, I was tasked with finding out what sort of penguin was a Penguin biscuit–type penguin, while the Creatives went back to trying to 'create'.

I walked to the local library a few streets away to learn about penguins. In the Reference Section I quickly located a fat tome called *Birds of the World*, found a desk, and began my search. I was surprised to find there were seventeen types of penguin, most of which bore little resemblance to the one on the biscuit pack – Fairy penguins, Humboldts, Chinstraps, Gentoos, Adelies... Ah, that's the one: Emperor penguins!

Back at the agency, I rang London Zoo and asked to speak to the head keeper of penguins. After a short explanation of why I was showing an interest in his charges, the helpful man invited me to come and view the creatures which had been such a large part of his life since leaving the army. A few hours later I was among the emperors enjoying their crazy waddling gait; I even managed to offer a small fish to one of them. They really were fascinating – black and white and strangely ridiculous.

"Would it be possible to film your emperors?" I asked.

"Sure, people do it every day."

"No, I mean could we take some to a studio and make them the stars of a TV commercial?"

After a short pause, the keeper's eyes lit up like headlamps. "I don't see why not, as long as I'm with them. They know me, and I think the zoo would demand I was there to look after them. Would your agency be prepared to... you know... pay me – that is, the zoo – a sort of fee? The zoo is always short of money for its vital animal conservation work, and I, well, you know..."

"Of course. No problem. We can work out a contribution to the zoo's good works, and a fee for you too, naturally."

Five months later it was mid-July, by which time the creative idea for the Penguin biscuit commercial had evolved, had been presented to the client and enthusiastically approved for immediate shooting. The TV Production Department had found a film director and crew and had hired a Soho studio. Everything was ready for shooting to begin the next day.

I had spent the previous twenty-four hours with the creative and production teams to make sure that nothing had been forgotten and that no loose ends were left dangling, so nothing could possibly go wrong on the shoot.

"You know what the Creatives are like," Paul explained. "Watch over them like an anxious mother.

"This is the way things work when we shoot commercials. We invest a fortune in strategic and creative development, add the cost of physically shooting the commercial, and then we add on a healthy profit margin for the agency before presenting the quote to the client. That way, if all goes well, we make some serious dough."

I nodded, slightly concerned about where this was going.

"But if we screw up," he continued in a warning tone, "we might make a loss, because the client has agreed a fixed sum, while we have to pay whatever it takes to complete the commercial. Just make sure everything goes smoothly tomorrow, OK? Even one extra unbudgeted day's filming and we might go into the red. Our end-of-year bonuses wouldn't like that, would they?"

The thought that I might be in line for a year-end bonus sharpened my attention to detail still further. And my nervousness.

After a long day of checks, I had a level of confidence borne of youth and inexperience. I felt good about the shoot, though I wouldn't have gone so far as to say nothing could go wrong. I was only a tiny cog in a big machine; the workings of which I still didn't fully understand. It was my first shoot, after all. But with all my attention to detail, I'd covered all the bases. Hadn't I?

I was the first of the team to arrive at the studio the next morning to be sure someone was on hand to receive the penguins. After twenty minutes, a large white van backed up to the goods entrance. When the rear gate was lowered the penguins, encouraged by their keeper, began to walk out in single file like well-trained Boy Scouts. I smiled at the sight of the ten birds waddling in step up the goods ramp, though something – I couldn't quite put my finger on it – was definitely wrong!

Then it struck me. The black-and-white penguins I had chosen for the shoot in winter were now... yellow and brown!

I guessed correctly: they had moulted their winter plumage. I was mortified. I couldn't imagine what would happen when Paul and the creative team arrived! I was all hot and sweaty and had no doubt my blood pressure had gone off the scale.

Whose stupid idea was it to use live penguins in the first place? I felt guilty already.

Half an hour later and I was in the middle of a council of war, with the agency and the production company trying to work out how the situation could be rescued. Paul was in no doubt: "If we have to wait five months for winter plumage, then reschedule the postponed shoot, then the post-production, re-cuts and client approvals, we won't be on air for a year at least. That means we've lost the business for sure."

"Excuse me." The zookeeper spoke for the first time. His worried expression suggested he was scared of losing his fee too. "There is a way. We could paint the birds. It would have to be water-based paints, of course, so as not to clog up their plumage, but it could be done."

"Fix it!"

I ran for the door.

Two hours later, we were ready to begin the painting. Unfortunately, it soon became clear that no one had explained the plan to the penguins. They showed us how fast they could run and peck with their sharp beaks, and I felt sure the studio's carpet tiles would never be quite the same again. Eventually, however, a modus operandi was established. One member of the crew would lay flat on his stomach holding a penguin's legs at arm's length, while a second crew member held the penguin's beak firmly closed, and a third applied the paint.

By mid-afternoon, the shoot began. There were minor teething problems, though, when it became clear that even with the help of the keeper, it was impossible to get a penguin to do anything it didn't want to do.

"Penguin, penguin, this way! Come on! Look, nice fishy! OVER HERE, DAMN YOU!"

Nevertheless, some progress was made and perhaps half the commercial was soon 'in the can'.

And then, during the early evening session, first one penguin keeled over and 'played dead', and then a second.

"Keeper, what's wrong with these damn animals now?" Paul demanded.

"Well, it is mid-summer, and under all these studio lights, they're probably becoming dehydrated. You know, like sunstroke. And I don't suppose the paint helps."

"Don't tell me the problem – what's the damn solution?"

"I suppose we could get them a kid's paddling pool or something like that, to cool them down when they're not on set."

"Fix it!" Once again I ran.

Ever efficient, within half an hour I had bought a pool from Hamleys in Regent Street and got it to the studio. The birds loved it and were soon happily splashing around. Except as soon as they waddled into the water ... the paint came off roughly from their waists down. (Assuming penguins can be said to have a waist, that is.)

It was not until a full two weeks later that the "Pick up a Penguin, a P.P.P. Penguin" commercial was finished. Soon thereafter it was publicly acclaimed a great success. Sales of the chocolate biscuit grew strongly. The client was thrilled and the agency saved the business – but at a very high cost. Two unscheduled shooting days had been needed, so I wasn't surprised when no bonus arrived in December.

Two years later, it was time to make a second Penguin commercial. The success of the first was sufficient for most in the agency to have forgotten the traumas involved in its shooting (and the loss of bonuses), but the creative and production teams still showed understandable nervousness. As did I.

It was agreed at an early stage that we would not write a script and expect the penguins to cooperate in its execution. We would simply hire an indoor swimming pool and let the penguins do what penguins enjoy doing most – swimming and jumping in and out, with children and adults joining in. If we shot enough footage of birds and humans happily swimming and generally interacting with each other, it should not be too difficult to edit the footage together to create a simple story. And since it was an indoor pool, we could shoot in winter when the birds' plumage would be attractively black and white. No more penguin painting!

I visited the pool in Edmonton, to the north of London. It looked ideal. There was a large tiled area on each side of the pool where cameras could move freely. There was nothing on the walls like posters or names we would need to mask, and even better, there was a water slide, inflatables, a wave-making mechanism, and other facilities that I had no doubt would delight the birds.

What could go wrong?

Penguins don't show excitement as children might, but after their drive in the zoo's van they seemed delighted at the prospect of swimming in warm water, and began waddling around at great speed in their new environment. Indeed, you could say they took to it like the proverbial ducks to water. For a while all went well and the cameras rolled steadily.

With time in hand, and looking for a little variation from what was already 'in the can', the director got two zookeepers to lift a penguin to the top of the water slide and simply let it go. There were cries of delight all round. Clearly, the penguin loved the experience.

But a second attempt with a number of cameras covering the scene didn't go so well. After his release at the top of the slide, the penguin's descent was held up by its wing catching in the safety rail, which almost tore the wing off.

Pandemonium ensued. The other penguins seemed to sense something was very wrong, and the human swimmers refused to continue, because the pool's water had taken on an unacceptably pink hue.

"That's a wrap, ladies and gentlemen!" shouted the director over all the commotion. "Time to go home and hope we have enough footage to cobble something together."

Two months later the new commercial was aired … again to general acclaim. After that day, "**Never Work with Children or Animals**" was a phrase I would have etched upon my consciousness.

Chapter 2

The Start of It All

The evening after the first penguin shoot, I had agreed to have dinner with my sister in Islington. I was looking forward to a relaxed chat about anything except penguins and advertising. I arrived just in time for dinner, to be greeted at the front door by my four-year-old niece.

"Hello, Uncle. What have you been doing today?"

"Painting penguins, my princess."

"Oh Uncle, you are so funny. But what have you really, really, really been doing?"

"If you want to know what I've really, really, really been doing, Sally, I've been painting penguins.

Sally ran crying to her mother. She never quite believed her Uncle ever again.

This wasn't the first time members of my family had wondered why I hadn't applied for a "real" job, in a "sensible" profession like the law or medicine.

As the son of a local government officer in rural Kent, I had an incredibly happy, if rather uneventful childhood. My primary school exam results got me into a competitive grammar school where I flourished – at least on the sports field playing hockey and as a bass guitarist in the school pop band. I managed to stay in the top stream for my schoolwork, but found myself close to the bottom of it most years once the end-of-term exam results were published. Being a Boy Scout filled most of my spare time - at least until girls appeared on my adolescent horizon.

I sat my "A" levels in 1964. I had no dreams of any particular type of career; in fact, I didn't have much of an idea where my studies might lead me. I reckoned it would be more a question of who would want to employ me, rather than what I might want to do. Not adept at maths or sciences, I found myself specialising in arts subjects by default. But what was I to do with a certificate listing Geography, History, English Literature, French and other similarly uninspiring subjects?

I wasn't really that ambitious anyway. If I could earn enough to be like Mr Solly, that would be good enough for me. A friend of my father, Mr Solly had retired after a career running a small department store in the neighbouring town of Maidstone. He lived in a large but not ostentatious house with a little under an acre of garden, which was kept tidy twice a week by a part-time gardener.

What singled Mr Solly out in my teenage mind was the fact that in retirement, he had enough money to go on holiday whenever he wanted to, and if he fancied, could buy a new car without having to do any financial planning or negotiate a loan. In short, he was 'financially comfortable' in a way my father could never have hoped to have been. To be comfortable like Mr Solly became my life's goal – for the next few years at least.

In my final years at grammar school, it became apparent that if I really concentrated on my studies I might – just might – be the first member of my extended family to go to university. But even if I could win a place, what on earth would I study? Talking to my friends, it became clear there was one subject that could just fit my qualifications and was very fashionable at the time too. So I applied to three colleges to read Sociology (without having too much of an idea what the subject was all about).

For reasons neither I nor my teachers ever understood, all three colleges rejected me without even offering an interview. I felt a bit crushed because it seemed university was going to be out of the question. In disgust, I spent the rest of the summer in France with some friends. Thoughts about my future would have to wait.

However, in my absence, my father opened a letter addressed to me from the Enfield College of Technology. The Admissions Director expressed his regret that I had not been accepted to read Sociology, but went on to explain that the college had applied to run a new type of degree course called BA (Hons) Business Studies - the first of its kind in the country. A little to the surprise of the college, its application to begin the course had been accepted for the coming academic year. So, if I would like to be considered for the Business Studies degree, he would in turn consider me – seeing that the college found itself with a course, but as yet no students to study on it. And the course was due to start in four weeks!

By return, my father wrote back in my name, accepting the place they had offered me (which of course they hadn't) and I started my Business Studies degree course three weeks later, with no idea of what he had let me in for. As it happened, I couldn't have picked a more suitable course if I had tried. Or perhaps I should say, the course was correct in selecting me.

In my second year I shared a room with a Sociology undergraduate, so I learned a fair bit about the subject I could have been studying. It didn't attract me at all.

Four years of study passed quickly, and once again I had to think about the next big decision regarding my future. As one of the first students ever to have graduated with a degree in Business Studies, there was no way of knowing what employers would think of a job application from someone like me. Further, "Enfield College of Technology" didn't have quite the zing of "King's College, Cambridge" either.

My parents were unable to advise me. My father had left school at fifteen and joined the Royal Navy soon thereafter. In one guise or another, he had worked for the government throughout his career. My mother similarly had had a basic education and worked in part-time clerical jobs.

Looking back, I only applied to an advertising agency because my lecturers at university told me not to. They explained I would be job hunting when the economy was on its knees. At such times, companies chop their advertising budgets to protect their 'bottom line', so advertising agencies suffer a loss of income and have to cut back on recruitment to save money in order to protect their own 'bottom line'.

Stubbornly, I applied to two agencies anyway. To everyone's surprise - particularly mine - I was accepted by the first of the two agencies after just one interview!

It had been up to me to make my own decisions about my future but as it happened, Fate made this and most of my future career decisions for me. He repeatedly did an excellent job.

Chapter 3

London, 1972–1974

There were certainly times I marvelled at just how good creative teams could be - somehow managing to produce a 'silk purse' of a commercial from a 'sow's ear' of a creative brief. It made me feel proud to be in advertising.

It seemed unfair to me that in market research exercises, most consumers claim they are largely unaware of and unaffected by advertising – even though it's clear from brand awareness scores and hard sales data that they are. But what to me seems even more unfair is their ignorance of just how much work goes into those 30-second, carefully crafted ads they see in the middle of *Coronation Street*.

I first felt a sense of pride in the run-up to the launch of the first "biological" washing powder, code named "Project Alpha". Paul and I visited the client's factory to learn about the "revolutionary nature" (the client's own words) of this new brand. We toured the factory with a man in a white coat.

"You see, the most common and difficult stains to shift are biological in nature," he explained. "Take blackcurrant juice stains, for instance. Ordinary powders won't shift 'em. So housewives have to soak them in bleach before putting the stained garments into the wash. Bleach can easily damage the fibres of a garment and it doesn't do the trick unless it's in a high concentration anyway, so frankly the best cure for a heavily stained piece of material is to bin it. However, the enzymes in this new product literally 'eat' the stains."

"What are the most common stains a biological powder can help with?" asked Paul. "After all, it isn't every day you get soaked with blackcurrant juice, is it? Biological powders will surely have to have a wider relevance than that if they're going to succeed."

"Absolutely! Housewives worry most about four common biological stains. The first is urine. A bit embarrassing and not often talked about, but we all have little 'accidents', don't we?" the man in the white coat suggested.

Paul and I looked at each other as if to say "Not me! Do you?"

"The second most common, particularly with babies and young children in the house, is faeces," the man continued.

Total denial and apparent incomprehension on the faces of the two childless ad men.

"The third is blood, either from a minor accident around the house, or most commonly from leaky sanitary protection products. Happens every day to most women... or maybe it would be more correct to say, it happens during many months to most women. Lastly, they worry about sweat stains – probably their husband's if he's a manual worker."

On the train heading back to London, Paul and I discussed what we'd learned.

"Sounds like a fantastic opportunity for the client, and for us of course," Paul suggested. "It isn't often I go to a product brief to learn of a real unique, demonstrable consumer benefit being offered by a new product. Think of the number of washing powder commercials you've seen offering 'whiter than white' clothes, without saying how or why that particular powder should work any better than the others. They're all much of a muchness and housewives know it, but this new biological powder sounds like a real breakthrough."

"Yeah, but who'd want to be in the creative team given a brief like this one?" I asked. "After all, the opening line of the launch commercial can hardly be something like:

'Ladies, do you worry about piss, shit, sweat and period blood stains on your clothes? Well, worry no more, because with new Alpha...'"

"You're right, but I'm pleased to say that's a problem for the Creatives, isn't it? After all, it's what they get paid lots more than you and me to work out. Let's go and have dinner in the restaurant car with a bottle of wine to toast their success, shall we? Our expenses will stretch to that. On second thoughts, maybe two bottles of wine would be even better."

The following day, Paul and I were with two creative teams in Sam's office for the creative briefing. I made a short presentation of the main points we had learned from the factory visit, passed over all the usual briefing documentation and invited questions.

Very much to my surprise, there were none.

A week later, we met again to review progress. Creative Director Sam looked unusually relaxed, even a bit smug, I thought, for someone who tended to burn up a lot of nervous energy.

"It's done!" he said. "We don't have a script yet, nor even a fully developed creative idea, but we've solved it! Give the client these four words and he'll wet himself: 'For Those Difficult Understains'."

Paul and I must have looked a bit bemused, so he continued: "We've added a new word to the language, you see – 'understains' – but it's one that needs no explanation and can be discussed without a hint of embarrassment. Most biological stains come from two parts of the body, but we don't need to say 'under-arm stains', or 'under-crotch stains' for that matter. Just 'Project Alpha for those difficult understains'." Everyone who does the family laundry will know exactly what we mean.

That evening, I took Ed the copywriter for a drink at the agency's favoured pub. I was fascinated by the creative process that had led to him coming up with the 'understains' idea. Or was it just lucky chance? A little to my surprise, rather than the self-praise or bull droppings I expected from him, he had a full and well-thought-through answer.

"As you know, we develop ideas in pairs – a copywriter and an art director. The theory is we work together; one of us thinking in words and the other in pictures and images. Sometimes it's a visual idea that comes first, so the copywriter has to fit his words to the pictures. Sometimes, as in the case of 'understains', I came up with words first and Jimmy has to suggest how a TV commercial or press ad might look when it incorporates those words.

"But Jimmy and I don't really work like that – at least not initially," he continued. "We always spend the first day or so alone. Only once one of us thinks he has something worth sharing do we sit together and work on it. As a copywriter, I can only work by myself, at least during those first 24/48 hours."

"So what happened with this project?" I asked.

"In this case, you came to us and said that the target audience was 'married women aged 24 to 48 with children'. Frankly, that's close to useless to me. I can't write words that would ideally reach 10 million women. Think about it: a 24-year-old graduate in London with one small baby doesn't talk like a 48-year-old scaffolder's wife from Glasgow with four children, and one more 'on the way'.

"You see, if I'm to write words that get through to the person most likely to buy the brand, I have to 'know' her. I have to have a clear idea of what she's like, what she thinks about, what her day-to-day problems and dreams are, so I can 'talk' to her... like, you know, on a one-to-one basis, on her terms, using her words. Just she and I."

"So how do you do that?" I ventured, genuinely fascinated.

"I started with the research you gave me. No point in me guessing more than I have to. The way I look at it is, if I could put these ten million women on some sort of graph or chart, who would be right at the centre? Of all of them, what would this woman who is most likely of all to buy this new washing powder be like?

"In this case Anna, (yes, I even gave her a name), is 30 and living in Birmingham. She has two primary school-aged children and a husband who has a junior management job in the local council. She got six 'O' levels and one 'A' level at school. She worked as an assistant at a local nursery school until she fell pregnant with her first child. She had felt a bit of a failure career-wise, but now that she's a full-time mum and housewife, she's much happier and more fulfilled. They are not rich by any means, but she's prepared to pay a bit more for a new product that offers a real benefit.

"It's so much easier to talk to Anna, alone, rather than to ten million of her sisters all at once! In my head, I sat with Anna – side by side rather than facing her, because I didn't want to interview her – and she described her life and eventually her laundry problems to me in her own words. It was Anna who found the subject of personal stains a bit difficult to put into words without embarrassment. She came up with 'understains', not me ... even though all this was happening in my head, of course."

Now that's *real* creativity, I thought.

Two weeks later, we presented a finished TV commercial script to the client. He was thrilled, though there was no evidence that Sam's prediction was correct – that he would be needing Project Alpha for his own underpants when our new word was revealed to him.

All too rarely, an outstanding copy line marries perfectly with an outstanding visualisation, rather than one being dictated by the other. For instance, one Land Rover commercial showed a very atypical commute. A driver in a business suit drives over very rough ground up to the base of a nearly vertical reservoir dam wall. He gets out and, with the type of gun used at sea, shoots a grappling iron on a rope up the wall and over the top. He attaches the free end of the rope to a winch on the front of the Land Rover, gets back into the driving seat, and winches himself straight up the wall. At the top, he drives onto a single-track road and accelerates away towards a major road.

This exceptional visual "commute" emphasising the toughness of the vehicle is married with an exceptional copy line:

Problems getting to work?
Land Rover.

The Best 4 by 4 ... By Far.

But never let it be thought that account directors can't be creative too – in a marketing sense, at least. An excellent example is the continued success of a megabrand called Brylcreem.

In the late 1940s, 1950s and early 1960s, there was only one fashionable hairstyle for the majority of men, virtually worldwide, and there was one dominant global brand, which provided it. Brylcreem. Men's hair was sticky with what would now be considered an excessive quantity of this product, making their hair shine under lights. It was pretty unpleasant to touch, and left stains on the backs of chairs, but no one cared – it was the fashion.

As often happens with fashion, things seemed to change, virtually overnight. Men suddenly wanted more natural hair in a style that would be a pleasure for a girl to run her fingers through – hair that was still under control, but looked and felt clean. Sales of Brylcreem plummeted, starting in Europe and North America, but moving like wildfire around the rest of the globe too. What should the account director responsible for Brylcreem do as he saw the sales of one of his biggest accounts collapse?

Could he get away with reassuring the client that all would be well if this 'temporary glitch' in sales was turned around by increasing advertising spend? That would be extremely dangerous, and at best, would be a short-term solution.

Instead, the agency's answer was to recommend a two-pronged approach to rejuvenating the brand. First, a new and quite different ad campaign was suggested to slow the decline: a campaign that emphasised how little Brylcreem was required to give attractive, controlled hair. The campaign, called "The Brylcreem Bounce", showed a man flicking his fringe, which moved up and down in a controlled but natural-looking way, as the jingle told us:

> **Brylcreem – just a dab will do yuh,**
> **Brylcreem – you'll look so debonair.**
> **Brylcreem – the girls will all pursue yuh,**
> **They'll love to get their fingers in your hair.**

What was being communicated was that Brylcreem was not part of a dead fashion – *it was part of a new one, if used in the right quantities.*

Still, more needed to be done. As usual, the agency fell back on market research - the trusted problem solver. It undertook a major study among a range of male respondents of various ages. Most, whether current or lapsed Brylcreem users, seemed to agree on the answer to one question:

If Brylcreem was a man, what sort of guy would he be?

Nearly all those questioned agreed he would be a nice guy — perhaps a bit middle-aged. He looked after his appearance and was proud of his good looks and fashionable grooming. Perhaps surprisingly, he wasn't a "stick in the mud" or old-fashioned, and he had many positive attributes.

Based upon these findings, the idea of creating a male grooming range was born.

While the brand name itself suggested it was suitable only for 'cream' products, the product development department came up with a whole range that would be suitable for appearance-conscious men, thus fitting what we had been told was a Brylcreem type of guy. First came a hair gel - the type of hair dressing that was pushing the older hair creams off the supermarket and pharmacy shelves. After all, they say: "if you can't beat 'em, join 'em".

Then there was a shampoo and a deodorant. A really with-it, modern brand for a with-it, well-groomed man! Now you can also buy Brylcreem Original Protein Enriched Hair Cream, Brylcreem Beard Oil, Brylcreem Extreme Hair Gel, Brylcreem Wet Effect Hair Gel, Brylcreem Strong Hair Gel, Brylcreem Protecting Stubble Oil, Brylcreem Hair Wax and Brylcreem Nourishing Beard Wash.

It is pretty obvious that the most valuable assets manufacturers of consumer products have are their brands. So it is the job of advertising agencies to advise their clients on how their brands can be kept up to date and relevant to end users. It is a job that never ends because consumers are ever changing.

A prime example of keeping a brand relevant to a changing environment was the need to change the slogan on all ads and packs of Maltesers. These chocolates were particularly popular among females, in part because of their commercials' tag line: "The chocolates with the less fattening centres."

One day, an MP stood up in the House of Commons and asked whether it was acceptable for a TV commercial to tell a blatant lie? How could a honeycomb made of sugar be described as less fattening?

The TV commercial was taken off-air that night just in case someone in government officially agreed with the MP and took action against the client. No one at the client end would have wanted to hear what the official government answer would be. Nor would they want to see negative PR in the newspapers thereafter. The slogan had to go... *and immediately.*

What to do? Would there be a need to change the whole positioning of this well-established brand and remove one of the key reasons women bought it? Or was there a new set of words that could be defended against further attack, but which would imply much the same as the old one? It was decided to try the latter approach.

Two weeks later, the TV ads reappeared with the slogan:

"It's the honeycomb middle that weighs so little."

Two years after that there was yet another ad campaign and a new slogan, which is still in use now – forty five years later:

"The lighter way to enjoy chocolate."

Once again, research showed the ads were continuing to give consumers a remarkably similar non-fattening message about their favourite chocolate. Subsequent market research demonstrated that as far as the prime target audience was concerned, the new, credible, and persuasive slogans said much the same as the original one.

Luckily, few people are ever aware of what is said in parliament, so no harm done!

Later that year, the same client posed another question.

Sales of chocolate bars were falling. In part, this was believed to be the result of consumers' increasing concern about the reported negative health effects of eating large quantities of confectionery. Many former customers told researchers they couldn't justify to themselves eating a big bar, so they'd switched to healthier snacks. Also, it became clear from sales figures that drops in sales were particularly occurring in the summer, on hot, sunny days when soft and sticky chocolate bars were less than refreshing.

After the war, most men had manual jobs, so putting a large chocolate bar in their lunchboxes made perfect sense. However, in succeeding years with more and more men having sedentary roles, where they perhaps would eat in a staff canteen, women were changing their purchasing habits and leaving large indulgent chocolate bars on the supermarket shelves.

A major off-site meeting was arranged when the client, some of the sales managers, the production director and the head of new product development met with the agency client service team and Creative Director to brainstorm a solution, or more probably solutions, to the many problems facing the brands. The combined result of the new strategy saw total chocolate sales tonnage *increase* for the next few years, rather than decrease, because of a fresh marketing approach. Its main elements were:

1. The launch of 'snack-size' bars, roughly two-thirds the size of regular bars, but for the first time sold in multipacks in supermarkets rather than confectionary shops, to try to minimise any drop in overall sales tonnage. Women bought them as part of their regular supermarket shop, telling themselves that, as the bars were smaller, they would be better for their families (while eating many themselves, of course). After all, what harm could these smaller bars do?

2. The launch of 'fun-size' bars - again sold in multipacks in supermarkets. They were just 14g each and were ideal for small children.

3. The launch of ice-cream versions of the major chocolate bars, plus cartons of milk, flavoured like the solid bars - both principally to counter the summer sales trough.

4. The launch of King-Size bars followed, once it became clear that there was still a significant number of male consumers who had no difficulty wolfing down 70g–80g of chocolate candy in one sitting - often buying their chocolate bars by the handful in petrol stations before getting back into their trucks.

In contrast, there were times when a client's total lack of understanding about the very basics of marketing made it hard to discuss how the brand could best be developed. If an account director had a better appreciation of available strategic options than the client, that was good. After all, advice is one primary reason to employ an advertising agency. Nevertheless, if a client lacks a basic knowledge of the ideas underpinning marketing, it's hard to achieve a meeting of minds.

I should explain that marketing is largely a post-war concept. In the 1960s and 1970s it became a very fashionable word, with many a Sales Director changing his business card to Marketing Director, without their role or approach to their job changing at all. I'm sure that this lack of understanding, caused many opportunities for brand development to be missed.

The marketing concept simply states that to maximise long-term profitability, brand decisions should be made, as far as possible, in the light of consumers' wants and needs. If you can, you should ask yourself what your consumers would prefer you to do when facing a major brand decision.

A clever example of this was a difficult decision made by the chocolate bar client. The price of chocolate beans had soared, so to maintain profitability, the price of the bars would have to be raised or the product made smaller. In a price-sensitive market, the decision was taken to make the bar smaller. But would it be best to make it shorter or narrower? Or to reduce its thickness, (known in the business as its 'bite height')?

Previous research indicated that an important part of the pleasure of eating these bars was the sensation of teeth breaking through a relatively thick layer of hard outer chocolate and then sinking through softer, yielding nougat and caramel. So the 'mouth feel' (the pleasurable sensation in the mouth) would be reduced if the 'bite height' was reduced. As a result the product was made shorter, while maintaining its thickness.

Sales were largely unaffected by this change, and profits retained, while sales of the main competitor fell – their bars now having a reduced bite height! The taste of these competitive bars had not changed, and at first sight they appeared to be the same size as previously, but their mouth feel had been damaged. They were simply not as pleasurable to eat. The competitor's sales fell, while our client's sales held up well.

Sometimes a failure to communicate with a client ultimately proves embarrassing. If you feel a client is slightly wrong, it is possible to "nudge" their thinking so they agree to a slight adjustment to their view. If you do so diplomatically, they might not even notice, or they might believe it was their idea in the first place. However, if you are sure their position is totally wrong, diplomacy might not be enough.

One of my early clients in the late 1960s began manufacturing colour TV sets. Colour TVs had become a status symbol for many families, but they were very expensive, relative to average salaries. Most families that had a set, would have acquired it via hire purchase or rental contracts. Outright purchase was unaffordable for the vast majority. My client sold very expensive, premium-priced colour TVs that not only had an expensive colour screen, but also a coloured cabinet. Instead of the standard black box, you could buy a red, blue, yellow, or green one to match your décor.

We recommended a campaign in the *Sunday Times* colour supplement, because clearly the ads had to appear in a high-quality colour medium in order to communicate the brand's decorative benefits visually. The profile of *Sunday Times* readers was also very much 'up-market', so these premium-priced sets would be affordable to many readers. The client disagreed. He explained that a retired neighbour had recently visited his home and commented favourably on his TV set. Therefore he wanted our ads to be targeted at old age pensioners.

I was speechless. I apologised for my need to visit his lavatory, where I sat and wracked my brains for a polite response. I couldn't find one, so apologised for my need to leave hurriedly. My account director would have to fight this battle!

Never let it be said that we ad men look down on our clients. Well, ... not all of them, ... and not all of them all of the time.

More seriously, many of my clients became close friends, and some were simply a pleasure to work with. A prime example was Andy, a guy I knew from my university days who joined a London-based brewery as Marketing Director, and immediately appointed me to handle his beer business.

On his first day at work, he was at a bit of a loss as to what to do because his predecessor was out of the office, so there was no one to show him around. Sensibly, he decided to pass the time at his desk reading through old files. He found the recipe for the first beer the company had ever made, over four hundred years previously. Recipe in hand, he wandered from his office into the brewery to introduce himself to the Head Brewer, and ask him what he thought of his historical find.

"Fascinating, Andy. I wonder what it tasted like. Tell you what, I'll make a batch in our test brewery and we'll find out."

Some weeks later, a panel of professional tasters sampled the new/four hundred year old brew. They loved it. A second, larger batch was made so that hundreds of beer drinkers around the country could add their views in a formal market research setting. Once again, the new brew received rave reviews – regular drinkers of the company's main brand preferred the new beer to their usual one by a factor of seven to three.

At this point, we at the agency were consulted because, rather surprisingly, this success gave Andy a big problem. Not only was the old recipe producing a beer that was preferred in taste terms, but it had a higher specific gravity (a higher alcohol content), but fewer calories, travelled better and thus had a longer 'shelf life', and was about 10% cheaper to make.

So what was Andy to do? Should he launch "the better-tasting beer", "the high-alcohol beer", "the beer for the diet-conscious drinker", "the beer that tastes just as you like it every time", or "the cheaper beer that saves you money"? Or maybe something like "the traditional-tasting beer served to English royalty for centuries"? Or some combination of these attributes perhaps?

We suggested that many of his potential strategies could safely be rejected. No man goes to a bar for an evening drink with his mates in order to keep slim by drinking a diet beer. That is not macho at all! We also discarded the "travels better" strategy because drinkers expect that any drink they order at their pub will be in prime condition, so the claim offered no consumer competitive advantage.

"The cheaper beer" sounded OK, but no one would select such a beer in front of his mates when it was his turn to buy the next round, especially as the difference would only be a few pence a pint, given that a large part of the cost of a beer is in packaging, marketing, overheads and tax. (Maybe a cheaper beer could be launched as a brand distributed in supermarkets only, and therefore drunk at home when a lower price was more attractive?)

We started our planning by looking at the competition, and what they were saying about their premium lagers:

- Stella Artois – Pay to get the best
- Beck's – Appreciate German quality
- Holsten Pils – Classic quirky beer
- Moosehead – Totally unbelievable Canadian beer
- Red Stripe – Be cool, discover Red Stripe
- Tennent's Extra – Well deserved, for special drinkers
- Löwenbräu – When you're this good, there's no need to shout about it
- Kronenbourg – Once you've drunk it, you know it's the one

And then there was the highly successful lager with a brand positioning the drinker was not really meant to believe at all:

- Heineken – Refreshes the parts other beers cannot reach

We began asking panels of lager drinkers why they chose their favourite tipple, but we had no clear leads, because surveys expect respondents to give a logical answer, when the psychology of visiting bars with drinking pals is extremely complicated. Logically, all the majority could say was simply that they preferred the brand they bought most often because of its better taste.

Unfortunately, we did not find out what the best positioning for the new beer should have been, because it wasn't launched. Budgetary problems led the brewery to cancel all development work, so I guess we will never know the answer.

Andy came to the agency to give me the sad news. That night we both drank a lot of beer but, as a sort of protest, we did not drink one of his brands. He and I are still close friends.

Chapter 4

London, 1974–1977

On the first day at my second agency, my predecessor showed me around.

"There's a lot going on at the moment, but I think I've left things pretty tidy for you. Our biggest client is nice enough... for an American. He's already signed off on all the creative work and quotes, so you just have to oversee the press shoot for Smartlook and the shooting of the TV commercial for Super-Longline. It should be a stress-free first couple of weeks for you really."

This big client was an American underwear company. Smartlook was an elasticated panty girdle designed to hold in the bits below the waist that might otherwise be prone to sag a little. However, the garment's main product benefit was that it was formed from a single piece of elasticated material that had been moulded into shape, rather than sewn together. So no seams were visible when it was worn under tight garments. No one would know what was under that clinging mini-skirt! The design of the launch press ad was amazingly simple: just four similar photographs of a model's rear, and a few words of explanatory copy under each:

- Photo 1 would show the model's bottom wearing her ordinary panties, flesh straining over the waistband and under the elasticated legs. Not attractive!
- Photo 2, beside the first one, would show the rear of the same girl in the same panties wearing a tight skirt, all seams and bulging flesh. Not attractive!
- Underneath these first two, photo 3 would show the bottom of the same girl wearing Smartlook – sexy!
- Photograph 4 would show the same girl in her Smartlook underpants wearing a tight skirt. Sexy, with no seams or excess folds of fat anywhere to be seen.

This would be my first underwear shoot, and that would require a few adjustments on my part.

First, I would have to get used to the fact that underwear models take off their clothes in front of strangers every day. It is just what underwear models have to do, but their apparent lack of modesty and shyness takes some getting used to. Second, while the models take it all in their stride, young men in their prime, with scant experience of beautiful nude women, are prone to stand and stare mutely, while surreptitiously adjusting their garments to hide their quite natural response to what they were seeing.

This became apparent within moments of my arrival at the studio when I was introduced to a six foot tall, naked blonde. For a few moments I found it was strangely hard to look her in the eyes, or even remember my name, while at the same time looking cool, professional, commanding, and nonchalant. I just had to try to focus on what we were there to do. Steely control was what was required!

The first shot was straightforward, or so I thought – the girl's rear in a pair of her own ordinary panties looking ugly. Easy... except it couldn't be made to work the way it should, whichever angle the photographer chose. She simply looked fantastic! Obviously, the art director who had chosen this model had not checked whether she had the necessary excess folds of flesh. The ugly bits Smartlook was meant to hide just didn't exist.

"I know," she said to me. "Come and stand in front of me, grab my waistband and pull my panties out towards you. It'll make the elasticated waist and legs bite into my flesh at the back and it'll look like I have bulges. The photographer can paint you out of the photograph afterwards."

I found myself stumbling forward as if in a dream. "How many young men have had a better offer than this at work today, even before their first cup of coffee?" I wondered as I placed my left hand on the model's tummy and pulled her waistband towards me with my right. "Don't look down! Don't look down!" I repeatedly told myself under my breath.

Two days later it was the shoot for the Super-Long TV commercial. After the Smartlook hitches, I looked forward to it with a strange mixture of excitement and dread.

Super-Long was a new product. The US client had sent the only three prototypes that were available to London from Chicago to be used in the commercial. Longline bras are designed not only to do what all bras are meant to do, but also to hold in place any excess flesh on the lower ribcage and upper stomach areas below the breasts.

The commercial idea was simple, with most of the thirty seconds taken up with an actress dressed in Super-Long, talking to camera about her wonderful new purchase. This time, I ensured the selection of a model was more carefully considered – the girl had to be big enough to benefit from the new longline design. When I arrived, all the preparatory work had been completed: lights, sound tests, even a quick run-through of the script. I joined the film crew beside the stage. The film director clapped his hands to get everyone's attention.

"Please, folks, remember we have only three bras to work with. If anything happens to the first, we'll move to the second, but if we go through all three, we'll have to postpone the rest of the shoot and wait for more to be sent from the States," the Director warned. "So be careful. We've only got one day of shooting to get this right."

The first few takes went without a problem, but then the cameraman called a halt. "I can see body make-up on the bra, just above the left cup. Looks bad."

A crew member went to find the second prototype. It became clear that this replacement bra, and also the third and final one in reserve, were two sizes larger than the first one. I found myself with the unusual task of screwing up tissues into loose balls and gently stuffing them past each cup's underwire so it looked as though the breasts more fully filled the overly large bra cups. Simply to make conversation with the model and to overcome my embarrassment, I mentioned that more tissue balls seemed to be required in the left cup as opposed to the right one.

"It's not my fault if my boyfriend's right handed!" she giggled.

Later in the afternoon, the film director was happy for the crew to have a tea break because he thought he'd only need a few more takes to finish. But after the re-start the cameraman called a halt again. "The longline bit is creasing badly. I guess Angie's rib cage is just too small to fill the larger sized bra completely."

The third and final prototype was brought forward.

"OK, guys. This really is our last chance. Can anyone suggest how we can stop it creasing like the last one? I don't think we can simply stuff more tissues up Angie's front. There will be a visible gap between the material and her body."

"I know what'd probably work." It was the wardrobe assistant. "If I go to that supermarket a few doors down, I can buy some aerosol starch. We can put on the bra carefully, I'll pin it down the back to make it smaller, and then spray her in at the front. In minutes it'll be like armour!"

"Sound's good. Let's try it."

Twenty minutes later the spraying began. As expected, once the spray had dried the longline area became rigid and was crease free. Unfortunately, the freezing spray had a second, unexpected effect on poor Angie, making her nipples stand out like door stops.

"Take five and we'll see if they'll go down," said the long-suffering director.

Those five minutes were followed by a further five, then another. Poor Angie was mortified.

"It's a wrap!" I was forced to say eventually. "We'll have to finish tomorrow."

After all the bums and boobs of my underwear client, I was happy to learn about some of the other clients who awaited my attention – like Bill Blake at Southern Pharmaceuticals.

Bill's company was planning to develop a new product similar to, but he assured me much better than, Vaseline petroleum jelly. But that was where he had a major problem. Vaseline was a mega-brand around the globe, selling by the ton in tiny little jars, no one was quite sure to whom, for... well... dry skin and chapped lips for sure, but it seemed unlikely there were enough chapped lips in the whole world to account for the quantity of Vaseline being bought internationally.

"Consumers are obviously using it for something else," Bill told me. "If I knew what, I could make that a big part of my product development, and thereafter, of course, the advertising. People seem to buy bloody Vaseline in vast quantities, though there's hardly any advertising in any country. And with no advertising, consumers must be buying it for reasons they've worked out for themselves. Not knowing is just killing me. And to think that right now, Vaseline has no significant competitors!"

"Shouldn't be a problem to find out," I reassured him, as he was beginning to sound slightly hysterical. "We'll design a programme of market research. We'll find out who is buying Vaseline and why. I suggest we start in this country, and then, based on what we learn, we can broaden things out internationally if we want to. I have a feeling some of the answers might be a little... personal and sensitive, so I suggest using psychologists to interview Vaseline users in private, in their own homes, on a one-to-one basis, rather than the usual clipboard-in-the-street, questionnaire approach. It'll cost more, of course, but we want the truth, after all."

A month later, people were being probed about their Vaseline habits. As the results were being gathered and analysed, I was gratified to see I had been proved right about the brand regularly being used for 'personal' tasks. Another use repeatedly mentioned, which no one had thought of, was for the lubrication of sewing machines, because oil tends to stain the material being sewn. In fact, all sorts of domestic lubrication, such as treating squeaky door hinges, were carried out with Vaseline because it was cleaner and non-staining. A few trends like these stood out, but I was amazed how many respondents used Vaseline to do things it seemed they could only have worked out for themselves. One in particular caught my eye.

"Well, we… uh… use Vaseline for, you know … sex."

"I see. May I ask precisely how you use Vaseline?"

"Yeah, well, we don't have no lock on our bedroom door, so when me 'usband is getting a bit frisky, I smear Vaseline on the outside door 'andle so me kids can't get a grip on it, and they can't come in and disturb us. Works a real treat every time, it does!"

As I have already explained, advertising agencies rely heavily on market research. We need to understand the consumers of our clients' brands as best we can, so we are able to position and advertise their products in the way that is most likely to attract would be buyers, and get them to purchase. Sometimes the results only confirm what we believed we knew all along. However, so often I am floored by what is said in group discussions or written on questionnaires by ordinary folk like you and me.

There was a little gem from one research project. Another client, Pepsi, was determined to better understand teenagers so its advertising approach to this prime target group would be more "cool" (or whatever word of approval teens were using at the time). Again, private interviews were conducted by psychologists. One teenage schoolgirl in Cambridge was asked if she was a virgin. Her response was simply: "Not yet!"

Another research project confirmed what many of us have observed. Mothers have two emotions that play major parts in their lives – guilt and worry. These emotions are experienced at the birth of their first child and never go away, or so it would seem.

We were researching mothers' views about chocolate bars, and specifically about giving them to their children. We were discussing Milky Way – "The sweet you can eat between meals without ruining your appetite." The chocolate bar's small, light, whipped centre made it ideal for small children when they wanted a "little something" between meals, perhaps after school, without removing their hunger completely... or that is what the advertising claimed, anyway.

One woman typified the responses of the whole group: "I feel guilty if I give my daughter a Milky Way because, whilst I think it's probably the most suitable choice for her, I know it's not her favourite, and she'd prefer me to pick something more ... well... exciting."

"So how do you feel if you give in to her wishes?"

"I feel guilty too. I know I should have given her a Milky Way, but I'm weak and give in too easily. So I feel guilty if I do, and funnily enough I feel guilty if I don't. And *still* I worry about what's best for her. I spend a crazy amount of time worrying, and feeling guilty. It drives me mad!"

I suppose that is understandable, but some research responses have no explanation I could discover.

One of our clients marketed a national brand of sliced bread. His major problem was that the main competitor in the same market in the UK was much bigger, more heavily advertised and promoted through all the major supermarkets. Mother's Pride seemed unassailable.

Research suggested that what consumers wanted most from sliced bread was freshness and the convenience of not having to do the slicing themselves, as well as bread that would not rapidly go stale. Clearly, Mother's Pride did all that pretty well, and at a price that was often a penny or two cheaper than our brand. In what way could we say our bread was better? How could we attack the competitor's dominant market share? Even its advertising emphasized the high-quality freshness of the bread, with a cartoon "Mother" flying in her animated helicopter from shop to shop to check her bread was as fresh as it should be by giving each loaf a little squeeze.

Under the circumstances, as Mother's Pride seemed to be everything mothers wanted, we decided to try a seldom-used type of market research – Problem Detection Research – to guide us in our search for a way to attack this market leader. Rather than asking housewives what they liked about sliced bread, we asked them what they disliked. What really got up their noses about the products?

Three predominant answers came back, whether the group discussions were carried out in Maidstone or Manchester, Guildford, or Glasgow. Overall, to our surprise, they weren't happy about sliced bread at all, even though virtually 100% of housewives bought it!

The first factor we should have seen coming. At the time, all brands of sliced bread maintained product freshness by wrapping the loaves in waxed paper, which was heat sealed at each end and along the bottom of the loaf. Women complained that once the seal had been broken at one end to use the first few slices, the seal along the length of the loaf tended to give way too, so keeping the bread fresh became a problem.

As a result, our brand – Home Pride - was the first brand in the market to replace the waxed paper with a continuous plastic sleeve that was permanently sealed at one end, and kept closed at the other with a wire closure. The first slices could now be removed without affecting the freshness of the remainder of the loaf.

A second major problem with sliced bread, it seemed, was that all too often there would be a large air bubble running part of the way through the loaf, so there would be a hole in a series of slices; not useful if you were trying to make a sandwich! The client had not realised this before, but assured me that with a minor change to the recipe and dough preparation process, this would not be a problem any longer with its loaves.

The other big issue with sliced bread was that it wasn't 'real bread' at all. It was not like the bread respondents' mothers had bought from the local baker; made with skill and dedication by a guy in a white apron who had been up half the night to have really tasty, nutritious, warm, fresh bread ready when the shop opened in the morning. Instead, they claimed that sliced bread was "steam baked" in massive factories, probably sited at the junction of major motorways so that great fleets of trucks could make their deliveries all over the country first thing each day. While the women we questioned were more than prepared to buy sliced bread because of its convenience, they felt a bit guilty about it because they should have been buying "real" bread.

They said that what they thought they ought to do was ignore the convenience factor and give their families real, nutritious, tasty, local bread each day, rather than mass-produced loaves of dubious food value. Some said that holidays in France had shown that French housewives had not fallen into this trap. They still had *boulangeries* in every village and bought their baguettes daily. British housewives should really do the same!

This key finding both amused and bemused our client.

First, the client assured us that there was no such thing as 'steam baking'. Today's sliced bread was baked in modern ovens, but the essential cooking techniques had not changed at all for centuries, aside from oil or gas being used as fuel rather than wood. Where did this common misconception come from? The same two words were mentioned in group discussions wherever the research was carried out, though 'steam baking' simply didn't exist, and had never existed. Sure, there was steam in the baking process – it helps in the crust formation – but no "steam baking".

A second misconception was the idea that sliced bread was mass produced in a few vast factories that were strategically sited to allow simple transport logistics. In reality, each of the major sliced bread companies had grown its national brands by buying up local bakeries, which, in the main, were still largely being used. With a few exceptions, bread was not baked in big factories at all. While nationally approved recipes were used in each branch, bread was still made by essentially the same bakers who had always done the job (or perhaps their sons and daughters now), and in much the same traditional ways.

These findings helped our client 'bite a large slice' out of Mother's Pride sales.

First, all its loaves were placed in the new seamless plastic sleeves. Second, we launched a new TV campaign showing how the bread was baked locally. Commercials showed the bakers – flesh-and-blood craftspeople, each with their town or city of origin printed prominently across the top of their white aprons – proudly discussing topics like new recipes amongst themselves. Each of the bakers was referred to by his first name and clearly took his skills seriously, bantering with colleagues from other towns about how *their* loaves were just a little bit more special, and it would be they, rather than any of the others, who would come up with the next new product idea.

In contrast, Mother from Mother's Pride was still shown in animated commercials flying around the country in her helicopter, which helped support the view that her bread was baked in enormous factories. One could say she flew right into our hands, particularly as her loaves were still wrapped in waxed paper.

During my second month at this agency, I had my first meeting with a company that made a range of sauces and condiments, but wanted our help launching an instant gravy – the type that accompanies England's most traditional dish, roast beef. As I knew from my own attempts at cooking, traditional beef gravy brands such as Bisto were not that easy to prepare. Mothers passed down their recipes to their daughters as though it was the secret of some magic potion, but all too frequently the results of my attempts were either watery or lumpy. If only a traditional-tasting gravy could be made as easily as instant coffee!

That's where 'Gravymaker' came in. A couple of teaspoons full of granules stirred into hot water was all that was needed for a rich, full gravy that would impress the most critical mother-in-law. No lumps... according to the client, anyway.

It was agreed to test-launch Gravymaker in only one minor TV region at first, rather than risk a national launch with all the possible costs in money and reputation that a nationwide product flop might inevitably cause.

So where to run the test market? The account executive tasked with suggesting a suitable TV area looked at existing statistics on regional beef consumption and found that it was the Scots who ate the most per head. Luckily, before recommending a Scottish launch for Gravymaker, I checked on the sales of products related to roast beef such as Bisto, mustard and horseradish.

There was no match! Scots obviously loved beef, but were not keen on roasts, or so it seemed. They certainly ate loads of beef, but not roast beef. I could not imagine why, so I telephoned a friend who was the chef at the Caledonian Club in London.

"Och, it's been like that for hundreds of years, laddie. Centuries ago, we Scots couldn't afford ovens. We cooked in pots, out of doors, over open fires. So, we tended to eat cheap cuts of beef and make stew, not roast beef. Today, we're nay so poor and, yes, we can afford ovens, but still the tradition lives on even now. Strange maybe, but it's true. You Sassenachs can keep your roast beef south of the border."

Eventually it was decided to run the test in the Tyne Tees region of northern England. Now all we needed was the TV commercial itself.

Like most good ads, the idea for this commercial was simple. An older, grandmother type, "Nana", would convince her sceptical husband, "Gramps" that, although she had always made real gravy the traditional way, she had just discovered Gravymaker, which was so easy to make and just as tasty as the gravies she had spent so much effort creating in the past. Gramps tried Gravymaker and enthusiastically approved.

After the client's approval of the launch recommendations, I gave the go-ahead for the TV production department to make the commercial. A casting session was arranged for the following Tuesday at the production company's offices on the fourth floor of a block of offices halfway along Frith Street in Soho, central London, so we could choose actors who would become Nana and Gramps.

That evening, I was just clearing my desk when the producer put his head around the door.

"The casting is done. We've found Nana and Gramps, though we interviewed fewer than half of the actors who wanted to attend the audition. There was a power cut that stopped the lift from working, and many didn't have enough puff to climb all the stairs to the fourth floor."

"Could have been a blessing in disguise," I suggested. "If our client is going to invest millions in making two unknown actors into household names, we wouldn't want them having heart attacks before he's had his money's worth out of them, would we? Seems like you've just invented the ideal selection test – if they can't make it to a fourth-floor audition, they're not fit enough, so they're out."

Like most major agencies, our big client accounts were mainly consumer packaged goods – anything from Cadbury to Kellogg's or Procter & Gamble. But we had one that was different. Officially called the Central Office of Information (or COI), it was a government client for army recruitment advertising.

I found the account unusually stressful for a rather unexpected reason. At the time, the IRA was highly active on the British mainland, with bombs being planted in shopping malls, a pub, and the financial district of the City of London. What better target could there be than the advertising agency that recruited the soldiers trained to fight them? And who better to kill than the account director on the army recruitment account, who happened to have an office at street level on Grosvenor Street in London?

On bad days, I could imagine one of the cars passing slowly outside pulling up as the passenger threw a bomb at my plate-glass window. But I was young, and things like that just didn't happen to people like me ... did they?

A big plus in handling the account was having a like-minded advertising professional as a client at the COI. Speaking the same language, we got so much more work done in record time. Too often, clients not trained in the mysteries of marketing and advertising would say unhelpful things like they had decided to reject an ad or pack design because "My wife doesn't like it" or for some other equally irrelevant reason. At such times, I was forced to try to find a polite way of saying that I did not give a damn what his wife thought. The press ad design was for a motorbike aimed at young adult males, not a blousy old trout three times their age!

So, my fears for my personal safety aside, the army account was largely enjoyable. Once my COI client and I had agreed on a course of action, it became our joint task to present to the guys in uniform – the ultimate decision makers. Every few months, six senior officers bedecked in medal ribbons, shiny badges of rank and red epaulette tabs (designating them as staff officers, it would seem) would arrive at the agency.

The presentations would always start punctually at 11 a.m. and would end by noon, when large gin and tonics would be served all round. Thereafter we would retire to one of the mews cottages at the rear of the agency that acted as our client dining rooms, to enjoy the efforts of our Michelin-starred chef: the meal washed down with an excellent claret, coffee, port, and brandy.

The colonels usually left perfectly happy at around 4 p.m., having approved the next campaign. Of course the commercials varied in their message, though all stressed two aspects of army life that appeal most to young men: the thrills of soldiering and the camaraderie of life when in close proximity to their mates. The first we called "The Work Bs" – Battle, Bangs and Brotherhood – which were invariably followed somewhere in the scripts by "The Play Bs" of Beer, Beach and Birds.

My first army TV commercial involved following a platoon of young soldiers training to fight with light weapons and tanks, with the support of helicopters. On the day of the shoot, the coach arrived at the agency at 6.30 a.m. sharp and we headed off to the army's training ground on Salisbury Plain. Immediately we arrived, the army personnel met a logistical problem. Everybody in the team – whether agency or production team – had to be given a rank.

Without a rank, the army does not know what to do with you. For instance, for meals, do you belong in a mess reserved for Other Ranks, NCOs, Senior NCOs or Officers? The creative director, film director and I were given arm bands designating us as captains, while the bulk of the crew were sergeants. The art director and copywriter were lieutenants, which caused great mirth at the expense of the poor sergeant major who had to make sure we came to no harm.

Steve, our art director, was a bit of a rebel, with a blue Mohican hair-do and a large ring in his right ear lobe. As a lieutenant, he had to be addressed as "Sir" by 'Other Ranks' and NCOs. Every time our career sergeant major had to do so, you could see the word "Sir" sticking in his throat, as though he found it extremely hard to pronounce.

That aside, all went very smoothly, the way one might perhaps expect from a trained and disciplined army. The men who would star in our little epic had been well drilled and had clearly gone through the motions we had planned for them many times before.

I even got an opportunity to drive a tank! To my surprise, the driver's seat was amazingly comfortable, whilst the engine noise was really quite muted, though I've a feeling I might have found the experience less enjoyable if I'd been going across really rough country under fire.

By 4.30 p.m. the film had been 'put to bed', and we headed back to the agency. I had enjoyed the day, but I decided a career in The Army was not for me.

Just as I reached the door of my office to head home, the phone on my desk rang.

"Sorry, I know it's a bit late, but have you ever thought of working overseas? You see, I have this great post in Singapore going begging which has your name written all over it. Deputy Managing Director, big international agency. Good salary, free housing, one month's annual leave, all paid for. And health insurance, sports club membership, plus, plus, plus."

I had not thought of another move, let alone to the other side of the world, but why not at least go to the interview?

"Give it a whirl," the head-hunter encouraged. "What harm can it do? It's a good career move and you'll get a chance to see a bit more of the world at someone else's expense, before settling down to be a boring London commuter for the rest of your life. The MD is in town next Friday. Shall we say 11 a.m. at the East India Club in St James' Square?

What did I have to lose?

By a strange coincidence, I had a second experience of the Far East that week. The New Bombay Emporium had asked for a presentation from the agency. Its business centred on selling oriental food ingredients to the catering trade. It now wanted to sell to ordinary retail consumers through the usual grocery channels, so it needed marketing, packaging, and branding advice and then a launch campaign. I went to meet the owner in north London.

"Tell me a bit about your business, Mr Patel."

"Well, sir, we are the largest importers of ingredients for the Chinese restaurants of this country. Just about everything they need."

"You have obviously been very successful," I probed.

"Oh yes, sir! Selling to Chinese restaurants is just the business we are wanting. They usually pay cash on delivery with bank notes taken from their back pockets! We've never had a bad debt in the twenty-four years we've been in business here."

"Presumably, with your background and delivery networks you sell to Indian restaurants too?" I asked.

"Oh my golly, no, sir! No Indian restaurants – that's not the business we are wanting at all ... I don't trust the buggers!"

Chapter 5

Singapore, 1977

As I walked down the steps of the plane in Singapore, I marvelled at just how much heat aero engines throw back, even when they are idling on the tarmac. But then as I walked towards the terminal at Paya Lebar airport, I realised the heat was not produced by the engines at all – this was the normal ambient temperature on the island. I later learned that since Singapore sits less than one degree from the equator, the difference between the coldest and the hottest months was just one degree centigrade, on average. And there are no rainy seasons either, just a heavy thunderstorm at around 3 p.m. on many days, rain the like of which I hadn't seen before. These lead to cooler, fresher evenings.

I felt I could really get to like the place.

I walked to the office next day to get a feel for my surroundings. Every other shop front seemed to be a restaurant. I had never seen so many in my life – road after road, eatery after eatery, and street food vendors too. If nothing else, I clearly would not starve during the next few years.

The agency was in a most impressive block. The Chinese Chamber of Commerce Building on Hill Street looked more like a Buddhist temple than commercial offices, with its traditional carvings, brightly coloured tiles, and red-painted, black studded, heavy wooden front doors. It stood immediately opposite the American Embassy. Quite a change from the "tastefully understated" offices in Grosvenor Street I had become used to.

My first day was a Friday, which was a special day for most of the staff. The Malays, as Muslims, left for prayers at a local mosque at noon. Meanwhile, for the Chinese members of staff, it was Fish-Head Curry Day. I was invited to join them on their weekly pilgrimage to the Banana Leaf restaurant on Racecourse Road, but I pictured small fish heads floating around in a curry sauce and did not fancy the thought at all.

For the next few weeks, I managed to find a reason for not taking them up on their kind weekly invitation to join them. But eventually the excuses ran out and I felt forced to go along.

Just how wrong could I have been for so long? Fish-head curry comprises one enormous fish head in a large glass bowl of curry gravy. The neck and cheeks alone are enough for at least two people, and it tastes out of this world. Even so, I could not quite forget my earlier reservations.

"Do you mind if I take the eyes?" asked Danny.

"No, no, please. Be my guest," I spluttered. I had adjusted my perceptions of fish-head curry, and for years after it remained my favourite local dish, but curried fisheyes? Nah!

A year or so later, I had the pleasure of introducing an executive from our regional headquarters in Sydney to the experience of fish-head curry. He was in Singapore for the first time, and just for the day. He told me that, as he had never been to Singapore before, he wanted to eat something typically "local". Before deciding what to suggest, I asked if he had already checked in for his return flight later in the day. He confirmed he had, and showed me his boarding pass. He was in 27C - an aisle seat.

This made up my mind for me and we left for the fish-head curry restaurant. He savoured every mouthful and sent me a telex of thanks the next day from Sydney. The last line of his message said simply: "Thank God for the aisle seat though!"

At the agency on my first day, the afternoon started with a full company meeting in the presentation theatre, with all the staff gathered to listen to Alan, the MD. He began by introducing me, to smiles and nodding heads all round. The rest of the briefing reminded me of my very first fateful meeting in London, when a creative answer to the Penguin biscuit problem had been desperately required.

"As you know, our largest client – or at least the one which should be our largest, if they would only give us more of their damn business – has asked us to re-launch their washing-up liquid. Unfortunately, Jim and the creative department have not come up with what we need yet, so I want each of you to spend at least some time this weekend thinking about what you reckon might work. It doesn't matter that you've never written a TV script before. We just need an idea for a script that we can knock into shape next week. You don't need the words 'Creative Director' on your business card to be creative. Let's get on with it, folks, and good luck! We'll meet again at 9.30 on Monday."

I had a couple of ideas I thought might work, though I wasn't keen to stand up in front of employees I didn't know, exposing myself (so to speak) to their critical gaze. Just my luck, when all were gathered for the Monday meeting, I was called first.

"Well, the commercial starts with a standard washing-up scene, a woman at a kitchen sink filling a plastic washing-up bowl with a mixture of hot and cold water. A squirt of washing-up liquid, and then..."

"Ah, that's interesting, but that's not how we wash up here," Alan interrupted me.

"Perhaps I explained myself poorly. After all, there's only one way to wash up wherever you live, isn't there?" I replied.

"Actually, no. To start with, kitchen sinks here don't have hot taps, and we don't use washing-up bowls. You wash up like this...

First, you take the plates from the dining table to the sink and pile them up. Then you scrape off, or maybe rinse off, the major left-over food bits and re-stack the plates. Next you take a cup and squirt a small amount of washing-up liquid into it, then add a little cold water. Next you dab a sponge into the soapy liquid and wipe the plates with it one by one – piling them up again – before finally rinsing them under running cold water to remove the suds. The items are then left in racks to dry. Might sound strange to you, but it works really well."

Red faced, I sat down and tried my best to seem invisible for the rest of the meeting. Clearly, there were more cultural differences to adjust to than I'd imagined. In fact, I learned of a second that very afternoon. An American electric drill manufacturer was to be one of my clients. I met the MD and the two of us went through the usual introductions.

"The best way to get to know something of my business is to visit one of our wholesalers," he told me. "My car's outside, so let's go!"

The wholesaler was nothing more than an ordinary-looking hardware shop, not the big warehouse I expected. Singapore is a tiny island, and I was to find many aspects of business there somewhat smaller than I had imagined after my British experience. We walked around the store and then had Chinese tea with the owner in his tiny back-room office. Back in the heat of the street, I was asked for my thoughts after visiting my first Singaporean wholesaler.

"The man's a complete idiot!" I began.

"Why do you say that?"

"He's selling your drills for a lower price than he's paying you for them. He must be making a loss!"

"No, Chow is a successful trader, pays his bills on time, and I have every reason to believe he makes a profit each and every year."

"But how is that possible?" I asked.

"You think about it. I'll ask you for your answer when we meet next week."

The question bugged me throughout the following seven days. It was impossible, wasn't it? If you pay 5x and sell for 4x, you *must* make a loss of 1x. Surely mathematics were the same in the East and the West? From my morning shower to my last cold Tiger beer in the evening, the question seemed to have no answer.

So it was with a measure of relief that the second meeting came around so I could find out how it was done – if indeed there was an answer – and be put out of my misery. As soon as the client had sat down, I had to admit that I had not solved the conundrum.

The slightly smug American gave me a superior smile. "There is a famous saying here about the Chinese: 'If it moves they bet on it. If it doesn't move, they eat it.' That's true of Chow, our wholesaler. It is standard practice here to buy on 120-day terms: that's to say, he takes delivery of my tools today, but only pays me in 120 days' time. Once he's got the drills, he flogs them quickly for whatever he can get for them. Then he takes the money and gambles with it – horses, mah-jong, anything that takes his fancy. He's obviously a good gambler because we've never had to chase him for payment."

A second local point of difference really amused me. Our chocolate client could not understand why sales of its products fared so badly in June and July. It clearly was not to do with the weather, because the temperature is the same all year-round. We did not need market research to find that out.

The answer was simple: June and July were durian season. Singaporeans and Malaysians are just short of addicted to this fruit, so their snacking habits switch from chocolate to durian as soon as the latter becomes available in the market.

For those not acquainted with durian, I have heard their smell compared – rather unkindly, in my opinion – to a Parisian street urinal on a hot summer's day. They are banned by all hotels and hire car companies because their aroma lingers for a very long time. But Singaporeans just love them, and I have to admit that, once you get beyond their smell, they are delicious.

Another local anomaly was a phenomenally successful product called 'Brands Essence of Chicken'.

To put it into context, Singapore has world-class hospitals and other medical facilities in general. It now can boast that life expectancy in the republic is higher than in any other country worldwide. Yet the Chinese still frequent traditional Chinese medical practitioners, and herbal remedy stores. I am sure that many of these treatments have medicinal value, but one would expect the beliefs in, and reliance upon these cures would diminish over time. Chicken broth – particularly broth made using black feathered chickens – is treated with utmost respect as an almost universal panacea.

To strengthen girls after their periods and women after giving birth, as well as anyone recovering from a major illness, chicken broth is definitely called for, and is a common gift from friends and family. Whilst Brands Essence of Chicken is a western product, its small glass jars offer an easy and portable form of concentrated "magic cure," so is ideal for gifting.

But surely, one might think, reliance on such cures would reduce over time amongst the highly educated population. For this reason, our client's sales budget for future years always imagined that the turnover of their essence of chicken would soon begin to decline. But it did not; sales grew healthily year on year.

I did have a lot to learn, but a few months later I was thrilled when someone else with even less oriental experience came publicly unstuck.

The occasion was the major annual presentation to a multinational toiletries client. Its lead brand was an expensive, top-of-the-range anti-dandruff shampoo. These presentations were always very important, setting the tone and strategy for the coming year, but this one was particularly so because I would be presenting to a new MD who had just flown in from London – a client who knew even less than I did about Singapore and Malaysia. Someone who might just want to stamp his authority on his business by appointing a new advertising agency.

So, I not only had to explain with particular care what a great job we had been doing for his business over the previous twelve months, but had to add all the whys and wherefores as well so he would fully understand.

Before I could move on to recommendations for the following year, the new MD stopped me.

"Are you telling me that, although Malaysia has a majority Malay population, which obviously speaks Malay, we only advertise in Chinese and English?"

"Yes, you see the Malays largely live in *kampongs* or rural villages, rather than towns and cities. They have much lower family incomes, and they shop in small local village stores that probably don't even stock your premium brands. They tend to prefer cheaper alternatives anyway. Frequently, they will use washing-up liquid or bar soap to wash their hair."

"I hear you, but it feels all wrong to me. We are turning our backs on over 60% of the population. It's their country, dammit! We surely shouldn't be completely ignoring the Malays, and I intend to prove it. Let's meet again in three weeks to review your recommendations for next year once more, in the light of some market research I plan to do."

Three weeks later the meeting eventually reconvened. It was clear from the client's demeanour that he was about to prove the know-it-all agency wrong. I could see him thinking: "I may not know much about this stinking hot country, but I do know my basic marketing, as this ad agency is about to discover."

After the opening pleasantries, he slammed a document down on the table, which he explained gave the summary findings of research that had just been completed "next door" in Malaysia. Then he let fly with both barrels.

"My research clearly suggests that, on average, Malays wash their hair *three times more frequently than the Chinese or Indians.* So not only are they over 60% of the population, but they use products like ours three times more often than the other races, AND WE DON'T BOTHER EVEN TALKING TO THEM IN A LANGUAGE THEY UNDERSTAND! I calculate that we've been wasting at least half our advertising budget for years, and no one has ever thought to question it. I am *extremely disappointed.*"

I was floored. I had met a number of women of all three ethnicities – in fact, my secretary was Malay and my housemaid Chinese – but I found it hard to believe the Malays were three times cleaner than the others. Yet research from a credible company said they washed their hair three times more frequently. I called an account executive over to me.

"Susan," I whispered, "please take this research report summary outside and read it from end to end, and then come back and tell me if it sounds right or not."

Susan slipped out of the room and the meeting continued.

Twenty minutes later, she returned. She sidled up to me, obviously finding it hard to hide her giggles.

"Are the conclusions of the research right or wrong?" I whispered.

"Can I tell you outside?"

I made my excuses to the client and went to talk to her in the corridor.

"Well, is the research right or wrong?"

"Both, I guess," she told me.

"How can that be?"

"The research asked Malay women how often they wash their hair, and the respondents answered truthfully, I would imagine," Susan began.

"Yes, and so?"

"The thing is, they should never have been asked such a question in the first place. They should have been asked: 'How often do you shampoo your hair?'" She giggled.

"Wash your hair or shampoo your hair, what's the difference?" I asked.

Susan calmed herself. "As you know, Malays are Muslim, and they're a bit, well, sensitive about... you know... anything to do with sex. Obviously, it's allowed between a man and his wife, but even then, it has a certain 'dirty' feel about it. So Muslim wives are expected to wash their hair once they've finished 'doing it'. Well, they're hardly likely to get out of bed, go to the bathroom (if their home has what we would call a 'bathroom', which frankly is unlikely in Malaysia) and go through the whole business of washing, drying and setting their hair all over again, are they? Particularly if their husband might fancy another bout later that night, or if they're going to have to get up early in the morning.

"I don't suppose their husbands would be best pleased either if they were forced to lose their beauty sleep as they waited for their wives to get back into bed after shampooing their hair," she continued. "So married Malay women have a small bowl of water by their bedside. After all the grunting and groaning, they reach across and splash a small amount on their heads. That way they can say they have 'washed their hair'. Ask a newly married Malay woman how often she washes her hair and she may well blush and say: 'Wah! Two or three times a night – most every night too!'"

I was tempted to announce these findings to the meeting, but I knew that would be the best way to make a life-long enemy of the new client. Embarrassing him in front of the agency team, and more importantly in front of his own staff, would have been a big mistake. So I suggested a coffee break and took the client to one side to explain.

The meeting ended soon after, and to my surprise and pleasure I received a letter by hand the following day thanking me and my team for our hard work, and approving all our recommendations for the coming year; even though I had yet to present them to him.

About this time, I began to realise it was not simply the advertising industry that could benefit from research. There were others who equally needed a better understanding of the general population in order to fine-tune their strategies before executing them. In this case, it was the Singaporean government that would have saved itself a lot of time, effort, and embarrassment if it had understood its citizens better before acting.

Singapore is made up of three main ethnic groups: Chinese (who are in the majority), Malays and Indians. The population is well assimilated, but the two smaller groups tend to live in certain areas of the island with their own places of worship, shops and restaurants. There was very little tension between them and their differences, such as holy days, were celebrated by all through common public holidays. However, in large part, each would speak their own language at home and in family-run businesses.

But the government decided to go one step further than simply encouraging cultural harmony. It wanted to develop a unique Singaporean culture that, in time, would supersede the current ethnically based ones. All citizens were asked to watch the television each evening so that they could learn "Singapore Dance Number 1, Number 2 and Number 3". Each dancer on screen wore a mixture of Chinese, Malay, and Indian dress (in other words, "Singaporean dress"), while the steps were vaguely reminiscent of traditional dances from all three groups mixed together.

We were then encouraged to learn Singapore Song Number 1, 2 and 3. In short, the government was attempting to create an artificial culture that it expected the population to immediately take to their hearts. In this way, citizens would begin to see themselves primarily as Singaporeans, rather than as members of a particular ethnic group living in Singapore.

Had the government first tested this strategy on a small group, it would have realised that cultures develop over centuries. They are not consciously designed to fit some predetermined government objective; they do not just "happen" over a short period of time.

In most countries, the government would have become a laughingstock in the local media after such a public failure, but open criticism of the ruling party simply did not occur in Singapore. After some months, the Singaporeans ignored the songs and dances they were meant to have learned, and the whole exercise was quietly forgotten.

However, the government tried various other social engineering exercises to encourage the largely compliant population to change in ways that were seen to be beneficial to society. Statistics suggested that the Malays tended to have larger families, comprising children who, on average, were considered under-achievers. In contrast, Chinese of marriageable age were not marrying in their late teens and twenties, but instead they tended to be either studying, developing their professional careers or both.

With no great subtlety, young Chinese undergraduates and graduates were given financial incentives to marry and have children. Dating clubs were started in colleges and universities, and the republic's total ban on pornography and erotic literature was relaxed... anything to get the pulses of the Chinese high-achievers racing. Once again, though, this social engineering strategy was largely ineffective.

Towards the end of my first year in Singapore, I found I had a hidden talent. I had been waiting half an hour at a recording studio for a voice-over artist to arrive to record a radio commercial for us.

The recording engineer wandered over. "Hey, you Ingliss, ri? Why not you do voice, lah! For you easy! Can?"

"Can. Or at least I'll try."

That was the beginning of a promising second career, except the recording fees would never make me rich. From then on, I found myself recording commercials in twos and threes for other agencies as well as my own. The other agencies would have had kittens had they known they were exposing their scripts to a competitor, but I guess they never bothered to ask whose voice was being used.

Many of the scripts came from locally owned and run agencies. I had great fun with their scripts because, while my voice was 100% genuine English, the words I was asked to record often were not.

"Siew Mun, I can't record this. It's gibberish," I complained having read one script. "Look, I understand I'm meant to be the expat manager of a trading company here questioning my shipping clerk over his choice of the Star Shipping Line for a consignment to Rotterdam. I mean, I get the point – I'm meant to be surprised because I don't realise that Star now operates between Singapore and Rotterdam. But I can't say: 'Chang, is it that I am to presume that you have chosen Star Shipping Line...'"

"Is bad Ingliss?" Siew Mun offered.

"Not exactly, but something like that hasn't been spoken by an Englishman since the last Queen Elizabeth was on the throne ... at least. The agency will look stupid. Not my problem, I know, but you've got to warn them."

Siew Mun went back to his control booth to telephone the agency. A few minutes later he returned. "No, they say it good Ingliss. Voice over man not to cliticise, lah."

"OK, but don't say I didn't warn them. Silly arses!"

Four months later, the Star Shipping Line was one of my clients. I never told anyone about my role in the downfall of their previous agency – and I did not feel even a hint of guilt.

To a British expatriate, adjusting to life in Singapore is not that difficult. After hundreds of years of occupation, the locals have got used to the funny *kwailohs* (long noses) and the *kwailohs* have got used to them. The greatest adjustment for me was having someone living in my bungalow with me.

Ah Kwai, a 64-year-old spinster, originally from mainland China, was my fantastic housekeeper, cook, shopper, laundry maid, caterer (if I had a dinner or parties at the house) and whatever else I might think of asking her to do for me. In London I was used to wandering around the house in just underwear, but now I had to think twice.

We only had the occasional difficulty. One evening I returned from an after-work drink with my boss Alan in the Great Shanghai Bar around the corner from the American Embassy. The Great Shanghai was totally above board, unlike similar establishments in Bangkok. In the 1970s Singapore was very strait-laced when it came to male-orientated establishments, and the Great Shanghai was no different from the others. The bar girls really were there to serve drinks and chat to clients, rather than provide other unspecified services.

After sharing some jokes with my colleague, one girl had said to me, "Oh, you so hamsap!" Back at home that evening, I related the story to Ah Kwai and told her what the girl with poor English had said while obviously trying to describe me as "handsome".

"No," said Ah Kwai with a little ice in her voice. "The word 'hamsap' is Cantonese. The best translation I can think of is maybe 'dirty old man'."

At that point she turned on her heel and retired to her room at the rear of the bungalow. I was glad to find that the next day she was back to her usual cheery self. Clearly, I had been forgiven.

Given the country's excellent education system and the focus on teaching English, language was usually no barrier. But Singaporeans do have a unique dialect, used even by the better educated, if only in fun. Known as Singlish, it includes common grammatical errors and the incorporation of Chinese, Indian and Malay words into an English sentence. Some of the expressions I remember are:

- "Heck it, lah!" – I don't care any more
- "I die already!" – I'm in deep trouble
- "I shag, lah!" – I'm so tired
- "Steady, lah!" – Yes

The government-run TV station did not allow Singlish in commercials.

However, some English usage can still raise a smile, like the food stallholder on the coast at Jurong who advertises his pork offal dishes as "Pigs Spare Parts", or the clinic whose name is "The Eastern Piles Clinic". ("How about my Western piles?" you might ask.)

My biggest challenge was not communication, but not over-consuming the excellent local cuisine, which (given the climate) is invariably eaten with large quantities of very cold Tiger beer.

Singapore was, and still is, a disciplined country – by no means a police state, but the control and "guidance" of the authorities cannot be denied. Whatever the disadvantages of this, the advantages are clear. With corrupt and economically struggling states to the north and south (Malaysia and Indonesia), few Singaporeans have reason to complain about their extraordinarily successful country, which can probably still boast the strongest currency in the world. Yet the tight control from above does create anomalies.

After a particularly long meeting with a client at the Singapore Convention Bureau, I suggested I buy two Big Macs for the client and me to share at the newly opened McDonald's restaurant nearby - the first in South East Asia. That evening I submitted my expenses for the meal. Two days later, a plain clothes policeman came to my office and gave me a formal warning about bribing government officials! No gift for a government employee, however small, was acceptable – not even a humble Big Mac, it would seem.

Chewing gum was banned because of the mess left on the streets, soft porn magazines were banned (for reasons unspecified), as were men with long hair, and roads could only be crossed on foot at designated places.

I complained to my client at Singtel, the government-run telephone company, about clicks on my home telephone line when

I dialled out sometimes. He suggested that complaining would not be a good idea, as they were caused by the authorities listening in to my conversations to ensure I had no anti-social plans. "They'll get bored and tap someone else's line after a while, so the problem will soon go away," he told me. He was right – a few weeks later it stopped.

The most amusing example of this rather heavy-handed approach to ensuring the population behaves occurred just before the opening of a client's restaurant; the first Shakey's Pizza Parlour on the island. The week before the opening, a health inspector called to check that everything fitted government public hygiene regulations. It seemed that according to these regulations, which had not been changed since colonial times, there needed to be one washing-up sink supplied with running water to service every so many tables.

A quick count by the inspector showed that there was only one sink, which was five short of the minimum allowed, given the restaurant's size. It would not be allowed to open until this was rectified.

Russ, my American client, explained that he didn't need extra sinks as he had installed two enormous, catering dishwashers loaded with detergents and disinfectants, which would be so much safer and more efficient than washing up in cold water, by hand, in open sinks that didn't need to have either detergents or even hot water. Moreover, all those sinks would take up too much space.

The inspector sympathised, but explained that regulations were regulations and he had no authority to bend them, however silly they might appear to be. (In this way, the government ensured that civil servants could not be bribed into allowing rules to be broken.)

Russ was angry at this nonsense, and his reaction showed it. He bought the requisite sinks and had a plumber pipe in cold water to each one. To show his displeasure, he had the sinks fitted six inches below kitchen ceiling height, so washing up would have been impossible.

The inspector was asked to call again. When he entered the kitchen, a look of disbelief gave way to a half smile once he realized what Russ had done. He opened his attaché case, pulled out the regulations, and spent some minutes checking whether the sinks had to be at a given height above the floor, or even a given distance beneath the ceiling, for that matter. Satisfied that there were no such restrictions, he counted the sinks and signed a certificate, which he duly passed to Russ. The restaurant opened the very next day.

One other memory of my time in Singapore continues to amuse me. I knew that a meeting with one local client was going to be particularly difficult. Quite simply, we had failed to do what we had agreed at the previous meeting, and I only noticed a few hours before I was due at their offices. The creative work was not on brief; quite simply, it was wrong.

Normally I would have telephoned to postpone the meeting, but for some reason I decided to brazen it out and convince the client that, on further consideration, we now felt the new press ad layout represented the best approach. Certainly, it would do the job, but .... A young trainee Account Executive fresh out of Singapore University came with me to this, his first client meeting. After leaving the successful meeting, I asked Louis what he thought of it.

"Oh, Sir, you lie so beautifully!"

Chapter 6

Indonesia and Brunei

In my second year in Singapore, my agency was asked by the government of Brunei to help it launch its first television station. It was to accept advertising, so advice was requested as to how this might best be done.

I was given the job. I flew first class to the capital, Bandar Seri Begawan, as a "Guest of the Sultan". While I was there I decided to call on the local Chartered Bank headquarters, because in Singapore the bank was a major client. We would have loved for it to use us as heavily in Brunei, even if a large budget there would be tiny by even Singaporean standards. The Chief Manager (Brunei) was an amiable man, but to my disappointment he seemed uninterested in running the types of campaign that worked so well in Singapore.

"How about trying to introduce the children of this country to the concept of saving, by handing out these Disney money boxes?" I suggested. "They are cute, it will give the bank good PR with the authorities for encouraging the savings habit among the young, and you'll have introduced the next generation to your bank, rather than a competitor."

"A good idea in theory, but our local retail business is tiny here, and you won't find a single major international competitor," he replied. "We are only in Brunei at all because it is a large oil exporter and it's we who handle the dollars generated. With our computers calculating in billions of dollars, do you really think I want to be opening piggy banks and have my staff counting out small coins?"

It proved not to be my most successful client meeting.

In the 1970s Brunei had no tourist industry to speak of, and only one place to stay, Brown's Hotel. Some local expats claimed that the name referred to the colour of the water dribbling from the showers. I doubted it, but the water in the bathrooms did fit the bill.

While at Radio Televisyen Brunei, I befriended a Welsh engineer from the BBC who was also helping develop the new station. I soon met his wife and seven-year-old son, who amazed me with his linguistic skills. At home, the family spoke Welsh. At school and pretty much everywhere else the boy spoke English, but when kicking a football around with his young Bruneian friends in the evening he spoke Malay. Somehow he managed to remember which language was the right one for each occasion, and never seemed to mix them up.

The other memorable event of my visit was also unconnected with my job. As there wasn't that much to do beyond work in the evenings and weekends, it was recommended that I take a motorised canoe tour of the interior, which included a one-night stay in a Dayak longhouse - large bamboo huts on stilts that accommodate a whole community. It was particularly recommended because the Sultan had paid for the installation of large TV monitors in the communal areas of each longhouse, along with a generator and aerial so that the Dayaks could watch his programmes.

The journey upriver was a little scary because it was a small canoe, and both the wildlife and water colour made an unscheduled swim very unattractive. I developed a deep respect for David Attenborough and other wildlife naturalists, plus their camera teams, who regularly make such trips with all the risks and mosquitos involved, to provide us at home in the West with a feel for life in these still partially unexplored places.

After half an hour or so I saw my first Dayak, fishing on the bank with a spear, and naked except for a loin cloth. The people seemed to have advanced little beyond the Stone Age, living with just the most basic of tools. On arrival, and having climbed up into the longhouse, I was shown to a small area of matting that would be my sleeping area for the night.

After a meal of very tasty grilled freshwater fish, I sat on the rush-matting floor of the common area and watched TV with the rest of the occupants. I could not get my head around what a mind-blowing clash of cultures I was observing. Those surrounding me had had no education (at least of the school-learning type we would all take for granted). They had only recently benefited from electricity – though that was only there to power the TV – and yet they were watching an episode of *Hawaii Five-O* on a giant colour TV. Prior to the arrival of Chinese traders and European colonialists, the Dayaks had not even got around to inventing the wheel!

On the TV screen I saw cars, motorboats, helicopters, telephones, and every imaginable modern artefact we take for granted. But what were my neighbours understanding when they saw the same images? It must have seemed like magic, or as science fiction might appear to Westerners. The dialogue had been translated into Malay (the language of the majority of the population of Brunei), but this was not a language the Dayaks could understand any more than the original English.

Not for the first time, I had reason to question the Sultan's priorities when deciding how to spend some of his billions of petro-dollars to help his rural subjects by giving them free TV sets. Perhaps it might have been better to start with schools and clinics. And would advertisers pay to have their commercials viewed by individuals with no money and no comprehension of the brands being advertised? Even had they had money and a desire to spend it on these brands, there were no shops for them to go to.

On my last day in Brunei, I headed to the airport and was personally guided to the first-class lounge. When boarding began, I was again personally escorted all the way to the plane; the ground stewardess holding my hand. Once we were airborne and

I was enjoying an excellent meal, a flight attendant came to my seat and held out a bottle of white wine and another of XO cognac.

"Would you like white wine or red, sir?"

"Oh, I think I'll try the red please." Their innocent charm and ignorance of alcohol had advantages; it would seem.

Another neighbouring country I was responsible for was Indonesia. I was not looking forward to my first trip after chatting to Sarah, an account director in the largest market research consultancy in Singapore. She had spent six months in Jakarta and had a series of horror stories of life there. One I remember was about a rather embarrassing itch and swelling she developed within the first month or so. She described her situation graphically.

"On the first occasion, I went to a doctor and told him the symptoms. He took one look at my 'bits' and diagnosed an infection which would require a course of antibiotics. After a few days, the symptoms disappeared, but the following week they returned. So I went back to the doctor. He expressed surprise and concern that I should have returned with the same condition so soon after my last visit. Then, he suddenly looked at me with an expression of growing shock and disbelief.

"You aren't taking baths here are you?" he asked. "Oh my God, never do that! Limit yourself to showers because the water runs off your skin in a shower. If you lie in a bath, heavens knows where the water might enter, and what harm it'll do. We may be in the capital city of Indonesia, but we are on the edges of civilisation here, and the tap water can be literally lethal, even if you don't drink it. Please, from now on, showers only. In any restaurant you don't know, don't drink water, or even have ice cubes. Drink beer or wine. It's more fun and so much safer."

I remembered this advice and decided not to trust any Indonesian restaurants so that I, too, would have to stick to beer. Such a shame!

After clean Singapore, Indonesia was such a contrast. In parts of the capital the street smells were really overpowering, the rubbish in the river unsightly and the bribery required to do almost anything in business was most unpleasant.

For example, only commercials actually shot in Indonesia were acceptable to the government-owned TV station for transmission.

It was necessary to have an official certificate stating that your commercial had been locally made. The problem was my Levi's commercial had been shot in the USA – the big give-away being the shots of the Grand Canyon. Even so, my local contacts knew how much to give to civil servants at various levels in the TV station's hierarchy, so within two weeks we had a certificate confirming the film had been shot in Indonesia.

Not only did I find bribery upsetting in itself, but working out who should be given what, at various levels of the government hierarchy, in order to get the desired result was complex, and the whole procedure took so much time. While we had lists and costs to get most things done, there were often times when I simply did not realise a bribe was necessary, but without it nothing would get done. I worked for an American company too, and it was strictly illegal to offer a bribe under the US Criminal Code. So I had to be "creative" when charging a bribe to my expenses.

A prime example of the problem was my return flight to Singapore after my first visit. At the door to the airport terminal stood a man who offered to carry my case and help me check in. I rejected the offer with a grateful smile.

Once I had arrived at the head of the check-in queue and handed over my ticket and passport, I was told that my name wasn't on the flight manifest, so unfortunately I couldn't fly. Would I like to be booked onto the first flight the following day? Only then did I realise I should have accepted the offer of help from the man at the door.

I had to spend an additional night at my hotel, and then return at 6.30 a.m. for the early-morning flight to Singapore. This time, I gladly accepted the offer of help at the terminal entrance and, believe it or not, my name was on the flight manifest this time, so I could get home. Once I had taken my seat on the plane, I began to wonder how airlines could operate out of Jakarta with so many passengers presumed not to have shown up for their flights. Surely I wasn't unusual in not understanding about bribery at the terminal entrance?

Fortunately, I found myself sitting next to a very pretty Indonesian girl in her late teens or early twenties, and we spent most of the flight chatting. She told me that her father was sending her to London to study economics. Perhaps fifteen minutes before landing in Singapore, she asked if I was British. When I confirmed my nationality, she asked whether I *really* had to disembark in Singapore, because she was scared about the prospect of studying in London alone, and would feel much happier if I would fly with her and help her settle into the scary city. She would pay for my return ticket and could give me a gift of £5,000 for my troubles. Or £10,000 – a small fortune in those days!

Clearly, almost anything is considered to be for sale in Indonesia for the right price - even me! Unfortunately, I had to decline her generous offer.

Strangely, my other clear memory of working in Jakarta was another occasion when I needed to fly back to Singapore. At the check-in (where I had been ably assisted by a man I had met at the terminal door), I asked whether the flight was likely to take off on time. I was assured that no delays were anticipated.

In the departure lounge I could see my flight on the display board, so I settled down to relax with a cold beer and a book. A few minutes later, I looked up at the board again and was disturbed to find the details of my flight had disappeared. Stopping a man in a Singapore Airlines uniform who was hurrying past, I asked if he knew what had happened to my flight. His only response before he rushed off was: "The usual!"

Thirty minutes later, the departure board was showing my flight again, and in due course I boarded. It was only then that I learned from a flight attendant that a row of seats in business class had been removed to accommodate a stretcher. It seemed that "the usual" started in an operating theatre at one of the Jakarta hospitals. After the initial incision, the surgeon could see the extent of the problem and, rather than attempt to fix it himself, would simply sew the patient up again and send him to Singapore on the next flight to be sorted out there.

Chapter 7

Chicago, 1979

After eighteen months in Singapore, my head office in Chicago invited me to spend two months there. It seemed that they had had positive reports of my performance to date in Asia and now wanted to evaluate my long-term management potential. They also happened to have a couple of advertising problems that maybe, just maybe, this young Limey could help them with.

It is hard for visitors not to be impressed by Chicago, and I was no exception. My hotel was on the lakeshore, from where I could see an expanse of water that just went on and on. I had read that this lake, like an ocean, created enormous storms with waves that could swamp even an unwary car ferry. Not something normally expected of a 'mere' inland body of water.

On my first morning, I trudged to the agency through a light snowfall. Later, we took lunch on the veranda of an open-air restaurant with the sun beating warmly down, but when I walked back in the evening, it was snowing again. I could see why I had been told: "If you don't like the weather here in Chicago, hang around because it'll soon change."

And then there were the enormous skyscrapers that stretched for miles. There was so much to impress me. But that evening I learned something less impressive about the other side of 'The Windy City'.

A car picked me up at 7 p.m. to take me to the agency president's home on the lakefront for dinner. As I got in the back, I heard all the door locks clunk shut. The chauffeur turned to me and said, "Whatever happens, *do not* unlock the doors until we arrive. And don't be shocked if I drive through a red light at a junction. David's got a nice place on the lake, but to get there we have to pass through some very rough parts of town. We may have Blacks trying to wrench open the doors when I slow down at an intersection, to get at you and any valuables you may have on you. And that's an experience you really don't want to have, my friend."

After that, I decided not to go for any late-evening strolls alone during my stay.

My other lasting impression of Chicago was just how parochial the people were, even in this major city. On Sunday morning the best-selling newspaper had been left outside my bedroom door, a great fat publication that must have given hernias to young delivery boys each week, simply because of its weight. (I wondered how many copies I'd be able to carry myself.) There was some international news on the first two pages and national news on the next couple, but all the rest was about Chicago and the surrounding state. I'd been told that the majority of Americans didn't have a passport at that time in the 1970s, and now I believed it. It seemed many – perhaps a majority – had never even left their home state and had little interest in what happened outside it.

On my first day at the office I was introduced to a number of highly intelligent Chicago MBAs, but time and again I was asked the same question: "What's it like living so close to Vietnam?"

After a while, I stopped explaining the expanse of the geography of South East and East Asia, and simply answered: "Well, if the wind is in the wrong direction, some days I think I can just hear..." World geography would seem to be missing from most school curriculums in the USA.

The jokes and sightseeing ended on Day 2. I was going to be asked to help arrange a shoot for a new motorbike commercial, but as the briefing unfolded I thought of the saying, 'It was déjà vu all over again'. The new bike was to be called Condor after the biggest, meanest bird in North America, a kind of vulture with a wingspan of up to eleven feet!

I felt obliged to tell the production team of the mental scars left by the Penguin commercials, and showed them the physical scar on my left buttock made by an Emperor who was upset at being painted. My story brought the house down. After all, someone else's discomfort is always highly enjoyable, and they loved my description of my first shoot.

"Great story, but we won't have that sort of problem," one of them said. "You see, Jethro the condor has been used in commercials before, so he's house-trained. He was hatched in captivity - he only knows humans. He's thirty years old now, he'll be no problem. We just need him to fly. He can fly in any direction he wants because we'll have cameras all around to catch his every movement. They aren't the most beautiful birds before they take off, but once they're up, they just glide on the air currents. It'll be a breeze – so to speak. We only need a few seconds of flight from him. What could go wrong, for Christ's sake?"

I wasn't convinced and that evening wrote on the production department's large, wall-mounted whiteboard:

NEVER WORK WITH CHILDREN OR ANIMALS

To meet our condor, a production assistant and I flew down to San Diego and took a cab to the zoo. After a little searching, we found Jethro sitting on his perch, looking pretty miserable. And not only miserable, but ugly. He might have appeared elegant when riding the air currents over the desert, but he was completely bald headed, with black plumage over the rest of his body, except for a white collar around his neck.

"As happy as a defrocked priest," I thought, "though, who knows, maybe a lady condor would fancy him!"

We found Jethro's keeper and began to discuss his starring role in the new commercial.

"Shouldn't be a problem," said Rick, the keeper. "We've never had him flying free like this before, but he always comes to me when I call. I'm like his mother, you see. We haven't had him in a helicopter either, but I don't see a problem. Oh, I should warn you, if he feels threatened, he'll do what condors always have a tendency to do – he'll throw up over you. You should know that condor puke smells really bad, so I suggest you don't do anything to upset him."

I was relieved to see just how simple the advertising idea was. The bike would tear across the Californian desert throwing up clouds of dust (easy), viewed by a condor sitting at the summit of a flat-topped mountain, or mesa, overlooking the desert plain (easy). The bird would take off and fly over the bike – easy, because if it flew in the wrong direction the film editors could simply cut together shots of flying bird and bike so it seemed as if the condor (bird) was sweeping approvingly over the Condor (bike).

Consciously, I knew there wasn't much that could go wrong, but even so, I wasn't wholly convinced. You just never know with children and animals, do you? After all, I'd been bitten once before, in a very real sense.

On the day of the shoot, Jethro, in an enormous cage, was lifted by Rick and me into the helicopter, which had landed in the zoo's staff car park. The mildly sedated bird managed to mix his usual miserable demeanour with a look of extreme boredom. The helicopter took off. So far, so good. Rick spent the whole flight talking to Jethro, who showed absolutely no interest in what his "mother" was telling him and seemed to make a point of looking past him out of the window.

It seemed no time at all before we were landing on top of a desert mesa and lifting the still terminally bored Jethro and his cage onto the mountain's flat summit. The helicopter left us. Rick opened the cage and after a minute or two, Jethro wandered out over the dusty ground, still managing to look intensely bored with everything around him.

Rick and I plugged in earpieces so we could hear the film director at the foot of the mesa.

"OK, in a moment I'll say 'Go bike'. I want to see the bike make some tasty twists and turns at around sixty miles an hour, clearly being ridden by the sort of guy all the men who'll be queuing to buy a Condor would like to believe they could beat. Then I'll say 'Go bird'. Rick, that's when you let Jethro go so that he flies down over the plain. OK, everyone, this is Take One."

"Go bike."

The rider managed some impressive manoeuvres, throwing up clouds of dust.

"Go bird."

Rick gave Jethro a bit of a push. The condor took a few tentative steps, stopped, turned, and walked back to Rick and me.

"Cut! OK guys, we'll try it again, only this time Rick, when I say 'Go bird', do you think you could give Jethro a bit of a kick up the butt for me? We just need him to fly, damn it!"

We had to wait nearly an hour for all the dust to settle and for the bike to be wiped down.

"OK, guys, we are all set for Take Two. Go bike."

As before, the rider made an impressive job of showing just what the bike could do.

"Go bird."

Rick gave Jethro a firm push and he headed purposefully towards the last rock, and then... disappeared over the edge. I didn't hear Jethro's less than elegant landing some sixty feet below, but when I crawled to the edge and glanced down, it was clear he wouldn't be attempting Take Three.

Later, in discussion with a distraught Rick, it seemed that Jethro's last flight had probably also been his first. The bird was so big, and condors have such difficulty getting off the ground (particularly after a heavy meal), that he had never had enough of a runway in the zoo, and therefore had probably never learned how to fly. There hadn't been the space, and the orphaned Jethro had never been able to watch an adult condor soar above him to show him how to do it.

The new motorbike was launched, on time, the following year, but with a different name. And a very different TV commercial.

The part of my advertising life I found most fascinating, wherever I was working, was learning about consumers, with all their strange habits and beliefs. They never ceased to surprise me. As they say in Yorkshire, "There's now't funnier than folk." Yanks were no different.

In 1970s America, smokers were really beginning to wake up to the dangers of their habit. The Chicago office had just helped launch one of the early low-tar cigarettes, with the expectation that smokers would flock to it. If they really didn't want to give up, or simply didn't have the self-control to stop, they could at least feel good about not doing themselves as much harm if they smoked this new low-tar brand. A low-tar smoker was a sensible smoker, right?

Wrong! The research showed the exact opposite. Some smokers did make the switch to low tar, but it seemed they actually felt bad about it rather than good, because they felt guilty that they had only partly given up their smoking habit. They felt that what they should really have done was to give up smoking completely.

The new brand of cigarette was like a "badge" displaying their weakness – their failure to give up – not their strength or good sense in reducing their tar intake. If they had stayed smoking their old full-tar brand, at least they would be showing a masculine disregard for the "good for you" lobby.

Strange, but true.

Chapter 8

Tokyo, 1981

While still technically on the staff of the agency in Singapore, I was tasked with setting up, and thereafter managing, an agency in Tokyo, until a permanent MD could be appointed to take over from me. It is a strange feeling when, for the first time, you find yourself with no one to lean on, no one to seek advice from if required. I couldn't remember 'needing' Alan, my boss in Singapore, for years, but I guess it had been reassuring to know he was there, and the responsibility, should something have gone wrong, would have been his.

Our HQ in Chicago had decided to form a joint venture in Japan to create an advertising agency in Tokyo that would be able to service our international clients' needs. The legal details had all been agreed before I arrived, but the joint venture was yet to fully function as an ad agency.

Our partner was a large company that ran a major retail chain of department stores, plus roughly a third of the Tokyo underground railway system. It wasn't my job to query this choice of partner, but one with no experience of running an advertising agency seemed a bizarre choice, to say the least - particularly as many local Japanese-owned agencies did exist. Surely one of them would have made more suitable partners?

To make my situation within the joint venture even more bizarre, most of the other employees spoke no English. My opposite number on the Japanese side was a sixty-eight-year-old senior manager from the railway side of the business, who had absolutely no English and no business experience that I would have considered relevant.

To this day, Japan is the most "foreign" country I have ever visited. Travellers still find getting around a challenge, but in 1981 no streets had visible names – in English or Japanese – to guide the pedestrian. Destination boards on railways and the underground did exist, but only in Japanese. I found the first two words I was forced to learn very quickly were (in both written and verbal form) "Exit" and "Gents lavatory". Without them, life on public transport, or in fact anywhere outside my hotel and office, really could be 'interesting'.

Four English-speaking account executives had been appointed, though their grasp of what was officially our common language was patchy, and their knowledge of advertising was non-existent. There were two other members of staff on my team who were clearly nothing more than "window watchers", but what they were meant to bring to the new joint venture wasn't clear. Once again, they spoke no English.

The concept of 'window watcher' had to be explained to me by an expatriate friend I regularly met in a bar near my hotel. A typical young graduate would join one of the major Japanese companies on leaving university and remain in its employ for the rest of his career. It was considered rather bad form to change companies, and in return, companies would not normally consider firing an employee, once his (and it usually was 'his', rather than 'her') knees were firmly under his desk.

Beyond that, promotion was nearly always decided by the seniority of the possible candidates. If you had been there longer than anyone else, the next promotion was probably going to be yours. Thus, if you were treading water, waiting for the next promotion to come your way, all you had to do was be suitably deferential to your superiors, bowing low if you passed them in the corridor, and do nothing for which you could be criticized. You had to just sit and perform whatever clerical function had been assigned to you, while 'keeping your nose clean'. That done, all you had left to do was to look out of the window – hence 'window watcher'.

This was seen as an inevitable part of the staffing overhead costs that were accepted as an unavoidable part of doing business in Japan. Before my visit to Tokyo, I had pictured the Japanese as a very efficient people, but the exact opposite is true – at least in the bureaucracy of office life. To succeed you had to (seem to) work hard by staying for stupidly long hours and not upsetting anyone. Similarly, holidays were frequently not taken. After all, if you did next to nothing, there would be next to nothing that you could be criticised for. And if you did not take a holiday, no one would become aware of what little you did. Also no one would realise that the company could easily operate without you.

There are norms like this that I simply had to adjust to. On the other hand, there were things that are so fundamentally unacceptable to an international company that they had to be changed, whether they were part of the local culture or not. I came face to face with one of these on my first day.

I had arrived early at the office – in part because I wanted to appear keen, but mainly because I hadn't slept well the previous night. The two female account executives introduced themselves and were already clearly very busy. Their two male colleagues only made an appearance an hour later. I noticed this happening on each of the first few days. After questioning one of the girls, I was horrified to learn that their punctuality was because it was their job to clean both the male and female toilets and prepare tea before their male counterparts arrived. It seemed that this almost universally happened in Japanese companies.

I decided there and then that, in this instance, the joint venture would not operate like other Japanese companies, and my first confrontation with the Japanese side of the management ensued. I insisted that the American side of the business would pay to have the toilets cleaned by suitably trained janitors rather than female graduates.

My demand was accepted with shrugs of incredulity since my determination that this should happen was not understood by the other side at all. Indeed, I wondered whether I had stupidly stuck my neck out over such an apparently small matter. The female executives concerned were grateful to me, but surprised I was so put out by their early-morning chores, which they had been perfectly prepared to do.

From then on, the men would have to make their own damn breakfast tea if they were thirsty – and if they arrived on time to make it themselves before the office officially opened.

(Funny people, these Europeans!)

At the beginning of the second week, I ran into a stupidity (or at least, what seemed to me as nothing short of a stupidity) that I had no choice but to accept.

On the first Monday of every month there would be a board meeting, which I would attend as the representative of the American side of the business. This would last for at least three hours and would be held in Japanese (which I didn't understand), except for my offerings, which would be in English (which most of my co-directors couldn't understand). As a result, there would be virtually zero communication between the two sides.

It should be remembered that only my side (which was just me) knew anything about advertising, so even if my Japanese colleagues understood English, they would have limited appreciation of what I was talking about. I asked the one director who did speak good English whether I could bring an interpreter to the next meeting.

My suggestion was viewed with incredulity. Was I suggesting that a non-board member would hear the highly confidential content of our meetings? Impossible! To find out what we directors had agreed at a board meeting, I had to wait for the minutes (which were in Japanese) so I could surreptitiously have them translated for me by an assistant manager at my hotel.

In the few months I was in Japan, I found myself learning how the country was different from the rest of the world, understanding those differences, and then trying to explain them to my European clients. I failed twice with my chocolate bar client.

The previous year the company had successfully launched a "good for you" chocolate bar in Europe. Given the extent of this success and the high cost of making different TV commercials for each market, it was decreed from the client's HQ in the USA that all markets would use the highly successful German TV commercial, suitably translated into the local language of course. If it was absolutely necessary, a new commercial could be shot locally, but it would have to follow the proven German format. After all, consumer concerns about good health were universal, weren't they? And everyone ate chocolate bars in the same way and for the same reasons, didn't they? What was wrong with using the same or a very similar highly successful commercial?

The German film showed a beautiful, slim, teenage girl eating the new chocolate bar in an idyllic lakeside setting. Seeing her, a shocked male companion expressed his surprise that she – a super-fit, health-conscious girl – would eat a chocolate bar. At this point she explained that she wasn't eating just any chocolate bar, this new one was made from healthy ingredients such as berries, yogurt, wholegrain biscuit, and nuts.

I spent an hour trying to convince my American client that this wouldn't work in Japan. I had been assured by my Japanese colleagues that the thought that a mere female would explain to a superior male what he should or should not eat was simply unbelievable. The script needed to be turned 180 degrees so that a handsome health-conscious male would explain the benefits of the chocolate bar to an air-headed female. Eventually, I succeeded and a replacement script was approved.

My victory was short-lived. The regional client came to Tokyo and vetoed our plans. The instructions from the US were perfectly clear. We would run the German commercial dubbed into Japanese. I did get the regional director to promise that if the launch failed, he would agree to do a re-launch using a TV commercial of our local design.

The launch went ahead... and was a complete failure. It was such a disaster that the retail trade was not interested in re-ordering more product for a re-launch. The brand had dug a large marketing hole for itself and had permanently disappeared from sight.

My second failure was even more serious, though to be fair it wasn't my fault and in no way was it blamed on me. One of my clients in Tokyo was a very amenable American. Dave and I got on well and spent many evenings 'drowning our sorrows' in local beer. Tokyo is ideal for the entertainment of young businessmen – local or foreign – and we bachelors made the most of it.

One evening, Dave told me that he was being posted back to the States and a young manager with Asian experience would be replacing him. I was sorry to see him go, but management rotation was practised by virtually all global companies, so this sort of thing was to be expected. I congratulated him on his promotion back to head office and hoped we would meet again in one country or another.

He left, and it was a full two weeks before I learned from a telex that his replacement was a guy with what was clearly a Chinese name. I immediately phoned Washington and asked Dave if the company was seriously considering using a Cantonese Chinese to run the Japanese office.

"Sorry, it wasn't my idea. I did tell them the Chinese hate the Japanese, and vice versa. After all, as they see it, the Japs are just the descendants of explorers sent out by one of the Chinese emperors centuries before. I explained about the Sino-Japanese War and the Second World War, the Rape of Nanking, and so on and so on."

"I've been told the guy will have a good supportive team around him, as I had had, and all will go smoothly," he continued, sounding unconvinced. "They reckon they were lucky to have an Oriental available to take the job, rather than ship over another American like me who would need to be 'broken in'. As far as the guys here are concerned it makes little difference whether Choy is Chinese or Japanese. They think Asian people are all much the same."

Even more seriously, I knew what the Japanese thought of the Chinese:- very inferior and far behind their Japanese cousins in terms of culture, cuisine, social development, industrialisation, and politics.

My prediction was that the Japanese would greet their new manager with smiles and bows. On the surface, they would do everything they could to make his stay successful and enjoyable, but then they would begin the process of making his life impossible. There would be nothing he could put his finger on, and nothing in writing, but he would be allowed to make inappropriate decisions, his briefings would be full of omissions, and decisions would be made behind his back. In short, his authority would be completely undermined. Unable to read or speak Japanese, he would be totally at their mercy. In the end, they would be "so sorry" that he had decided to leave.

He lasted a full 10 weeks!

I thought convincing clients was difficult, until I had to deal with our own company's president.

It was decided he would fly into Tokyo for an official signing ceremony to mark the new joint venture. My local Japanese colleagues were excited by the prospect. Our president was to be met at the airport by their president and put up in a special corporate guest house near the Emperor's Palace. That evening there would be an elaborate banquet. After the signing the next morning, the honoured guest would play golf with the presidents of both the railway and retail sides of the business, while their wives would all go out for sight-seeing and retail therapy. The second night would see another major banquet.

I phoned the president in Chicago with the good news.

"You are f*****g joking, aren't you? First, I'm flying alone – I'd have some difficulty explaining these arrangements to my wife at this stage in our divorce proceedings. Second, I've an important meeting in Hong Kong the next day, before dropping down to Sydney to try to sort out the fine mess they've got themselves into Down Under. What you're suggesting just isn't going to happen. Book a meeting room at the airport for the signing and lay on a bottle of bubbly or something, then I'll catch the next plane to Hong Kong."

I tried to explain the concept of "face" to get him to understand that as far as our new colleagues were concerned, he would not be taking them or the new joint venture seriously enough. They would therefore 'lose face' because Hong Kong and Sydney would be seen as clearly more important in our president's eyes. And even if in reality Japan was less important, how could he be so rude as to let his new partners realise it? They would view his few hours in Japan as a serious slap in the face.

"Could you perhaps delay the meeting until you could spare a few days in Tokyo, maybe over a weekend?"

"No bloody way! I hate Japanese food at the best of times, and all this bowing and scraping is just a stupid waste of time. The Japs are going to have to join the twentieth century sometime. After all, they've only got about twenty years left!"

The following day I explained to my Japanese colleagues my president's itinerary and regrettable lack of time in Tokyo. The icy silence was palpable. Eventually, only one junior Japanese executive "was available" to meet our president at the airport. The meeting lasted half an hour.

Just how strange the Japanese appear to other cultures was illustrated over a beer one evening when I was chatting to the one English-speaking director. A Japanese would never invite a colleague – particularly a foreign one – to his home. A restaurant or bar would be appropriate, but no colleague would be invited into a home. Nevertheless, I was curious what a typical middle manager's home would be like, so I asked for a verbal guided tour.

At the end I noted that he hadn't described the kitchen, so I requested some details.

"I don't really know," was the answer. "There are some white-fronted cupboards and stuff, but that's all I can tell you really. I never go in there."

"But if you fancy a beer, or a snack of some sort, you must go in there and know where to look for them!"

"No. I just call for my wife or daughter to get them for me."

A similarly strange element of modern Japanese culture is golf. I was repeatedly asked if I played the game. There was universal surprise when I said that I didn't. Later I learned that for junior and middle management in Tokyo, 'playing golf' meant being a member of a local driving range, because membership of a real golf club in or near the city was far too expensive for anyone without a very comfortable salary. Each of my colleagues had spent a fortune on clubs, gloves, shoes, cap, bag and all the rest of the golfing paraphernalia, but had never actually set foot on a golf course.

However, they all 'played golf'.

Chapter 9

Bangkok, 1982–1984

My career in advertising – in fact, my whole life – seems to me to have been a series of largely unplanned strange beginnings. Like my first day in Bangkok.

I had flown to Thailand to take up my new job as managing director of one of the major international advertising agencies there. Until then, having been a deputy managing director with a competing ad agency in Singapore for over five and a half years, it seemed as though I'd never be promoted to the top slot. My decision to leave was made for me when my boss Alan bought himself a new racing dinghy and moored it at Singapore's Changi Yacht Club. He clearly had no plans to move from Singapore to let me take over his comfy padded seat in the large office at the front of the Chinese Chamber of Commerce Building. And, after five and a half years, I felt ready to move on anyway.

As I left the airport terminal, I had my first experience of the Bangkok I came to love ... and hate. It was *hot*. Being March, and in the dry season, there were no clouds in the sky and no chance of a cooling shower. After disciplined Singapore, here taxis and cars were cutting each other up to get into a prime position on the ranks.

The air was full of dust and general pollution, long before air quality became an international talking point. This was the everyday chaos of Thailand. I had heard Singapore described by a critic as "a bit like living in a hospital". If that was true, I didn't dare to think what living in Bangkok could be compared to. Was this where I would have to live for at least the next two years ... or more?

The queue for a taxi seemed to snake in front of me forever, so I shared a cab from the airport to my hotel with a German businessman who'd been just ahead of me in the queue. He introduced himself as the International Sales Director of the company that marketed 4711, the big eau de cologne brand. After an introductory chat, he elbowed me in the ribs, and challenged: "I bet you can't guess in which country we sell the most eau de cologne."

"Germany?"

"No."

"France?"

"No."

"All of Europe?"

"No, but now you are trying to cheat, I asked which country. Try again."

"OK, the USA?"

"No."

"I give up."

"It's Saudi Arabia."

"You're joking! Surely they're not that bothered about personal freshness."

"They aren't. They drink the stuff! It's potable alcohol, you see. Saudi is the only country in the world where we sell eau de cologne in litre bottles. I must admit that when I first found out about it, I did try to sample some myself... but I think I'll stick to schnapps."

The hotel on Sathorn Road was an oasis of calm and blessed air conditioning after the streets of the capital. Checking in was easy and I was escorted to my room by a polite and helpful bellboy. This was more like the life I had become used to in Singapore.

As I unpacked, there was a timid tapping on the bedroom door. Five minutes earlier, I had telephoned the front desk to ask for a razor to be sent up; my hurried packing in Singapore had been just a bit too rapid, and I would need to shave before going to dinner. I wanted to give a good impression, after all. Following an interview in London, I had been appointed Managing Director Designate (Thailand) and was preparing for the first meeting with my predecessor, who would be teaching me the ropes over the next seven days before leaving to return to London. I thought I'd better look the part.

There were further hesitant knocks on my door. The opened door revealed a petite Thai woman, maybe in her early twenties, dressed in what could perhaps best be described as a green and yellow tennis dress. In one hand she held a sponge bag, and in the other she waved a razor expectantly.

"You wan?" she asked hesitantly.

"Yes, thanks. That's just what I need."

I reached out for the razor, but my visitor swept past me into the bedroom, before turning sharp right into the bathroom. I stood in the doorway to watch as she laid out the contents of her sponge bag beside the sink, and began running the hot water.

"Scuse," she said, gently pushing past me into the bedroom to collect the dressing-table stool and carrying it into the bathroom in front of the sink. Placing a towel on the stool, she indicated I should sit.

I wanted to explain that all I needed was the razor. I had learned how to shave myself and had more than fifteen years of practice, but my knowledge of Thai didn't stretch that far. Indeed, "please", "thank you" and "good day" were my current limits. "Oh well," I thought, "this might be a novel experience. I've never been shaved before."

I sat in front of the sink. She unbuttoned my shirt and pulled it down to my waist. This was all very new to me, and was... well... rather pleasant.

The shave went smoothly. She couldn't have claimed to have had my fifteen years' experience, unless she shaved her teddy bears in her crib, but she was skilled enough to do a good job – no missed tufts and absolutely no blood to be seen anywhere.

As I sat checking her handiwork, she quickly packed her bag and headed back into the bedroom with the dressing-table stool.

Buttoning my shirt, I joined her to see that she was sitting on a corner of the bed, apparently waiting for me. She asked me a question in Thai and offered a very big smile. I was lost. With no idea what she was saying, I assumed she must be waiting for payment.

I nodded, smiled and offered, "Yes, yes thank you, that was excellent. You did a good job. How much do I owe you?" I moved over to the bedside table for my wallet.

At that she giggled, kicked off her tennis shoes and began to remove what few clothes she was wearing. In short order she was walking around to the head of the bed and pulling down a corner of the sheets. She leapt in and sat there smiling, obviously waiting for me to join her.

Once again, I was faced with a communications dilemma, and this time my Thai really wouldn't stretch to it. If I called Reception, how would I have explained the naked girl in my bed in English?

"Oh, damn it," I said to myself, taking the easy (and I was sure the more enjoyable) way out. "In for a penny, in for heavens knows how many Thai baht."

I took a little longer to cast my clothes to the floor than she had done with hers, my shaking fingers not being up to the job of undoing the shirt buttons I had so recently done up without difficulty. To my amazement, I found myself just a little shy before her gaze.

During the next forty-five minutes or so, there were many things that surprised me. To begin with, I had never before been to bed with anyone who did that sort of thing... professionally. I expected a matter-of-fact acceptance by my partner of what was about to befall her, but instead she was all wriggles and giggles. Wasn't it me who was meant to be enjoying myself? Unless she was a brilliant actress, she seemed to be having a ball ... so to speak!

And then the strangest thing of all. After a wonderful "no holds barred" experience, she shyly emerged from the bed, grabbed a towel, ran to the bathroom, showered, and began to dress - just as I remember my sister having done on the beach at home in England years before. After wrapping the towel firmly around herself, she turned away from me and shimmied a little awkwardly into her underwear.

I couldn't understand the sudden coyness, but over time I came to appreciate that Thai "professional" women like to at least feign shyness. They may have sex with strangers for money, but they still considered themselves 'ladies' who should behave with decorum, and therefore should be treated with respect.

Having watched her dress, I reached again for my wallet. "How much do I owe you?" I asked, taking out some notes and offering them to her. Quite simply, I had no idea what the going rate might be for a shave, plus an exhausting work-out.

She giggled and reached for two 500-baht notes, put her hands together and bowed in a traditional "Wai" of thanks, picked up her bag and ran for the door.

I had just paid a little over £16 for a shave and an experience I certainly wouldn't forget in a hurry.

I dressed smartly for my dinner with Andrew, the current managing director of the agency I was joining, and went down to the bar behind the reception area to await my host. My choice of attire was my first mistake. Thailand is very much a casual country, and I could see I was over-dressed because Andrew arrived in denim shorts and a flowery, colourful shirt. I clearly had some adapting to do.

Looking back, I believe that Andrew's intention that evening was to shock me with a very extreme experience – extreme at least by the standards I was used to – just to see whether I was likely to 'survive' years in Bangkok. I later learned that many people didn't survive, particularly those who had brought wives with them.

After a few Singha beers, a short walk saw us entering a rather dark restaurant. What was most noticeable about the establishment was the fact that it was very narrow, with only space enough for tables to be placed against the walls to the right and left and a narrow corridor down the middle between them for customers and waiters to move from table to table. The largest party size the restaurant could comfortably accommodate was, therefore, just two, if customers were to talk to each other between mouthfuls. Guests sat side by side, staring at the blank wall in front of them as the busy waiters passed behind.

The menu was all in Thai and, knowing little about the cuisine, I suggested Andrew did the ordering. He had a smattering of the language, though he cheated by choosing food by pointing at photographs of the selected dishes. The ordering complete, we discussed our careers for a while and Andrew answered some of my basic questions about the agency. He then took me a little by surprise by asking:

"Are you a betting man?"

"No. I think gambling is a bit daft. You either wager a small amount so that, win or lose, the end result matters little. Or, if you gamble a lot, you spend your time sweating and nervously waiting for the outcome, which too often results in handing over more cash than you can afford. Gambling has never been one of my weaknesses."

"Well, how about a little bet with me? I bet you 100 baht that once our food arrives you will smile within the following thirty seconds. Come on... that's less than £2!"

"OK, once our food arrives, I will not smile for thirty seconds."

It seemed a childish bet, but why not? And why risk disappointing my host? Could it be that hard to keep a straight face for thirty seconds?

Some minutes later, a waiter arrived with the first of our dishes and I sat stolidly looking at the blank wall in front of me. I was determined to win.

"I will not smile for thirty seconds. I will not smile for thirty seconds," I whispered to myself, and just stared with a fixed expression.

Then the totally unexpected happened. Underneath the table, I could feel hands on my knees, gently pulling my legs apart as they headed slowly north towards my fly zip, which was gently lowered. I pushed the exploring hands away. This was just too much for one day. If this had been a test, I had failed. And I had probably lost my bet as well.

"Ah, you smiled! That will be 100 baht please!"

As you might expect, I have little memory of the meal we ate that night, nor of our conversation. Later, looking around the restaurant, there was no hint that it offered such unusual "dishes", though once I did see a customer choke a little just as he had placed a forkful of meat into his mouth. As they say, "Don't be eaten with your mouth full"… or something like that.

As in Singapore and Tokyo, I had to adapt to working in Bangkok. Singapore and Thailand were neighbours but culturally very different, in part because one had been a British colony for centuries, while the other had never been colonised. Many said that Singaporean Chinese had only one true religion – money – while Thailand was devoutly Buddhist. Chinese businessmen in Singapore, and throughout South East Asia, invariably drank beer or expensive cognac at dinner (the latter ruined, in my opinion, by adding ice and water), while the Thais drank beer or local whisky.

Wherever expatriate business executives find themselves running a company overseas, they obviously must ensure that the office is run on international lines using international systems and expertise, like all the other national branches of their global organisation around the world. After all, that is one of the key reasons they, rather than a local manager, are in charge. However, it is equally obvious that local cultural and religious practices must be respected and sensitively incorporated into the operation whenever possible. The MD must be prepared to learn and be flexible as well as teach.

I was to learn that over 90% of Thai men become monks at some time in their lives, giving up their families, careers, hair, and worldly interests for months at a time. In my second year, my studio manager, Somchai, was out of the office for six months for this very reason. A request for extended leave without pay might be inconvenient if the executive concerned held a key role in the company, as Somchai did, but a refusal would be impossible to justify, at least in the eyes of the staff. In contrast, Japanese executives – particularly window watchers – would never ask for an extended leave of absence for fear that the employer might find it could manage perfectly well without them.

Prior to Somchai's departure I had decided to remodel the offices, ending up with larger presentation theatres for client meetings. Once this was completed, I was advised by my General Manager, Khun Vivat, that we should have the offices re-blessed and re-consecrated by monks. If we didn't and ill fate fell on the office, the staff would blame me for my lack of foresight, respect, and faith.

A team of monks was invited to come to the offices to 'do their thing'. During the chanting and flicking of holy water liberally around the building, I saw a monk who looked vaguely familiar. Then it hit me. It was Somchai! He was hard to recognise because of his shaven head, saffron robes, and lack of beard, but it was him for sure.

I later learned the story behind his desire to spend a period as a monk, begging daily for food and divorced from the pleasures of the outside world. Months before, he and his oldest friend had taken a river taxi home after a night out. They were life-long neighbours and had played together throughout their childhood. During the journey, the helmsman had taken a corner too sharply and tipped some of his passengers into the water. Somchai's friend was never to be seen again.

It seems that Buddhists believe that while you live, good deeds are noted in your "book of life", and over time you build up a collection of "merit points" for these good deeds, which will assist you in the afterlife. However, it is possible to donate your points to another person, and in this case Somchai decided to give his collection to his dead friend – thus he was spending six months of contemplation and good works to increase his point count as far as possible, before giving them all to his dead friend to improve his experiences in the afterlife so he would gain a swifter re-birth into a good home.

That's what I call *real* friendship.

After my arrival, one of my first tasks was to attend a meeting at the US Embassy which was a short walk away. As the Managing Director of a US owned company, there were a number of American laws I had to obey, it seemed. I had to sign a declaration that I would neither offer nor accept any form of bribery. This I was happy to do because, after Indonesia, I disliked this common Asian practice in all its forms. However I signed the form with my fingers crossed – mentally at least.

I knew from my previous experiences in most Asian countries that bribery was so endemic that to do business at all involved at least a low level of bribery to be accepted. I comforted myself in the fact that I would certainly not offer a bribe myself, even if I accepted that at times the expenses claimed by some of my senior staff might seem particularly high to mask a bribe. Could it be that their receipts from bars and restaurants were as high as they were because they needed to "cross a client's palm with silver"? I did not want to know.

Just as in Japan, when faced with cultural and operational differences between Western ways and local ways, an expatriate manager must decide which local differences they can accept and which must be sacrificed to the company's global operating procedures. I ordered three changes to the decisions my predecessor had made before I joined.

Firstly, I changed the way the agency celebrated 'Sanook' - a traditional Thai concept that is untranslatable, but maybe approximates to "celebration" or "time out". When we won a new client, we had to have an hour or two of Sanook. Snacks, bottles of beer and Thai whisky would appear as if out of thin air and everyone celebrated. It would be inviting bad luck not to mark such an occasion in this way.

However, I noticed that even when we lost a client, it seemed Sanook was definitely called for as well. When I enquired why we were celebrating a client loss, I was told that no one particularly liked the client, so we were better off without him.

Then there were birthdays to be celebrated, and with 134 staff they came around very frequently. In fact, there seemed very few occasions on even fewer days that could be deemed unsuitable for a little Sanook.

This I couldn't accept. Alcohol was forbidden in the agency's offices worldwide, even if my predecessor had allowed it, but I imagined the negative reaction there would be in the office to an outright Sanook ban. So I decided on a good old British compromise. I announced that Sanook was OK at the agency as long as celebrations didn't start before 5 p.m. That left the risk that a visiting member of the international directorate might object to alcohol on the premises, but I could argue that the drink had been bought by the staff and only consumed after official closing time, so they were effectively drinking their own beverages during their own time.

My international colleagues would have viewed my second change as a backward step. Worldwide, in major Western agencies, all executives are required to fill in time sheets - which are universally hated. By calculating the total number of hours spent on any one client, management can work out the profitability of a client's business above or below the norm, and could perhaps cut back on, or increase, the services provided, or even fire the client if it regularly represented a loss. However, getting everyone to fill in the dreaded time sheets punctually each week, and then have someone consolidate all the data and draw conclusions about client profitability, took a huge amount of work in every agency I'd ever visited.

On my first day as managing director, I noticed that a young graduate sitting in a back room was surrounded by piles of time sheets. On the walls around his desk were charts and graphs showing his calculations of hours worked, by client and by department, and how they related to income from the client.

It was all very impressive, until I asked what comments or recommendations he had recently made to my predecessor about client profitability. None. He hadn't seen that as part of his job. He just did the calculations and passed them over – conclusions based on them were outside his job description. How many decisions had the previous MD made based on his calculations? None that he knew of.

The very next day he joined the other graduate trainee Account Executives working on client business. (He was thrilled until he learned he would now not need an office to himself anymore.) I saw no point in creating data that we didn't act on. In a small office like ours in Bangkok, it would take a very blind MD not to know instinctively which clients produced the best profits and which were "also rans". Even the revenue from the least profitable one covered some of our fixed running costs, so firing them wouldn't improve our bottom line. If I had no plans to fire any clients, I wouldn't need to waste the time of all members of staff to calculate how profitable or unprofitable a client was.

The decision to scrap time sheets went down rather better than the announcement of time restrictions to Sanook. The time-sheet statistician was a bright young man and I hoped I'd be able to find others like him in the future.

To help make sure that I could, I wrote to the local universities and the offices of our competitors to explain that in the autumn a new, free evening class in marketing and advertising would be taking place at our offices each Tuesday evening, and asked for applicants. Fifteen people turned up for the first lecture, plus 8 from my staff. The numbers gradually increased as the weeks went by. In this way I was able to evaluate each student and offer the most promising ones a job when I needed to recruit – a sneaky but effective way to identify the best local talent: even those working for my competitors.

Finally, I noticed that all staff, even directors, had to sign-in on arrival each morning. This seemed to me totally inappropriate for highly educated and trusted staff who, more often than not, worked well beyond the official hours without overtime payment. So I abolished clocking-in because, as I announced in a staff meeting, they were adults, and adults should be trusted and treated as such. This also went down particularly well with the staff, as (perhaps surprisingly) did absenteeism. Of course, some took advantage of this new relaxation, but they were few (and they were noted).

Unfortunately, not all my changes went so well. Beside my desk there was a wooden table of the type one might expect in a standard European dining room, and six straight-backed wooden chairs. This was not my idea of a suitable environment for important discussions with staff or clients, so I ordered that the dining table and chairs be replaced with easy chairs and a low, smoked-glass coffee table.

I was very pleased with my decision, until the new furniture was used for my first client meeting. After the usual introductions, a knock on the door heralded the arrival of our tea. Siriporn, our tea lady, began to behave very strangely. Holding her tray with cups and other tea things in front of her, she dropped to her knees and crawled over to us with her head as low to the floor as she could manage without scraping her chin on the carpet – or spilling the tea. What was she up to?

My secretary later explained that, according to Thai customs and beliefs, a person's spirit was to be found in their head, so heads are the most revered body part. To show due deference to her boss and his guests, she had to keep her head below ours while delivering the tea. As we were sitting just a short distance above the floor in our low-slung seats, her flexibility and gymnastic skills were stretched to the limit. She later threatened to resign if the old furniture was not reinstated, because her back couldn't take any more of this type of punishment. The new furniture simply had to go.

Siriporn obviously forgave me, because I was invited to be guest of honour at her wedding a few weeks later. To me, the sole European, the event was rather puzzling and frankly a little boring. After the meal, various relatives were handed a microphone and I imagined each was speaking fondly of the bride and groom and wishing them well.

Eventually, the mic was passed to me; clearly, I was being invited to say a few words. I've spent much of my working life making presentations, so this shouldn't have phased me, but as I got to my feet a stray thought had me in giggles. I realised I could say *absolutely anything* and be rewarded with smiles and applause. I rejected the temptation to recite the infamous poem "The boy stood on the burning deck" and briefly said what I thought was expected of me, before sitting down again to polite clapping.

I found it fascinating to observe how my competitors adapted to life in Bangkok. Firstly, the Managing Director of the agency JWT behaved in the way I observed a number of Americans to do. He never really settled into Thai life and culture and would only eat at American or European restaurants – partly convinced that he wouldn't enjoy all the yucky foreign spicy food, and partly through a fear of the level of hygiene local restaurants might practise. Sadly and ironically, he was shipped back to The US after just a few months suffering from Hepatitis B!

Then there were the "Scandahooligans" – men from Norway and Sweden who threw themselves wholeheartedly into all that out-of-hours Bangkok had to offer. Perhaps because of the high price of alcohol in their home countries, they seemed determined to soak up as much as they could during their stay in Thailand. This was apparent via their after-hours behaviour.

The saddest expatriate group was the Japanese. Their workaholic culture meant they arrived early each morning, usually 6 or 7 days a week, so that they would be at their desks should their bosses make an early phone call (Japan being two hours ahead of Thailand). Similarly, they would be in the office late … just in case! I have no reason to believe they were more productive than the rest of us; they just felt the need to *seem* to be more committed to their companies and careers. I found it easy to believe that "Karoshi", or death by overwork, was a real risk for them. As was a very frustrated and lonely wife who saw little of Thailand, or even her husband.

My first experiences of Bangkok's "comfort industry" confirmed its international fame as a bachelor's paradise. During the Vietnam war, when thousands of US servicemen visited the city for R&R, the number of establishments serving their twilight needs increased many times over. In my job, they were an essential and expected part of entertaining clients. Also, it was amazing how many international vice-presidents from our Head Office in the States felt the need to visit our small office each year, when the much larger Singapore and Hong Kong offices were regularly missed out of their travel itineraries.

However, during the early 1980s this industry fell on hard times. Firstly the GIs stopped arriving because hostilities in Vietnam ended in the mid-1970s. Secondly, the first global oil crisis had the Thai government restricting the opening hours of massage parlours to save energy. This was first announced on

TV when a friend and I were in a bar after work one evening. "I wonder whose energy they're trying to save?" he asked me innocently.

The biggest blow to the sex trade was the international spread of AIDS and herpes. Initially, the government denied there was any problem in Thailand at all. During a rare press interview, the Thai queen even bizarrely announced that there couldn't be a problem in Thailand because there was no sex industry in the kingdom!

Some months later the authorities changed tack and emphasised, in the local and international press the nature of the extreme measures they were taking to ensure these international scourges could not enter or spread in Thailand. Sex workers had weekly blood tests and establishments would be enforcing the mandatory use of condoms. The threat didn't go away, but it was at last being seen to be taken seriously.

Mike, my Regional Managing Director, had lived in the region for decades, and knew his way around the bars and massage parlours of Bangkok like a local. During our first evening out together, he obviously thought he should 'show me the ropes'.

"I don't know what you plan to get up to when you are off duty - and I'm not going to ask - but let me introduce you to something". He guided me into a supermarket.

"Nearly all drugs can be bought without a prescription in Thailand. The government reckons they are expensive enough without patients having to pay medical fees to a doctor for a prescription as well. This is one medicine I want to introduce you to. It is called 'Rifadin'. It's a broad-spectrum antibiotic which will clear up virtually any unwanted infection you might pick up. Oh, just one warning about it – it turns your urine a bright, almost fluorescent orange colour, so don't pee in front of anyone. They'll think you are going to die or something."

Two months later having applied to join the British Club, I was sitting on a bar stool waiting to be called for my interview with the club's committee. Another applicant came to the bar and we chatted as we waited. He told me he headed-up a pharmaceutical company which distributed drugs throughout Thailand.

"Which products do you distribute."

"A wide range, but the biggest seller is 'Rifadin'.

"Oh! What is Rifadin used for?" I asked innocently.

"Well, the W.H.O. say it should be reserved just for a very few serious conditions such as meningitis and leprosy so that resistance doesn't develop, but I'm afraid the main problem it cures here is various forms of venereal disease."

When he said he didn't have an advertising agency, I passed him one of my cards and made an appointment to meet him.

The next day I telexed my boss Mike in Hong Kong. "We have been offered the Rifadin account. Any comments?"

He replied within minutes: "Suggest we handle on a barter basis".

Danger often has a funny side and a type of gallows humour developed. On my third day at the office, I had to visit the company doctor. It seems that before being given a work permit in Thailand, a Thai doctor must confirm that the foreign applicant is sane. Our doctor, Richard Dixon, had been a Bangkok resident for many decades; many affectionately referring to him simply as "Doctor Dick the dick doctor".

As I sat in the waiting room I saw Jim, our creative director, leaving the consulting room. We nodded to each other as he passed.

"I believe you are seeking a certificate certifying you to be sane. What profession are you in?" asked Doctor Dick when I sat down in his consulting room.

"Advertising."

"Advertising! And you expect me to say you're sane!?"

Five minutes later I left with my certificate. Back at the office, I searched for Jim to see why he had been consulting Doctor Dick, and to check that he was OK.

"Yeah, I'm fine, but I had a bit of a scare. You see, a couple of weeks ago, I developed a bit of a... let's call it a 'dribble' and soreness, so I thought I'd better get it checked out. After all, my wife couldn't understand why I seemed to have gone off her. Doctor Dick took a sample of the offending fluid with an earbud and sent it off for analysis. I went back today for the results."

"So what was the verdict?" I asked.

"With a big smile, Dr Dick said to me: "She gave you 'head' didn't she?" "Seeing as you mention it," I told him, "my girlfriend

was a bit overly affectionate a few nights ago. How did you know?"
"Because your little fella has got streptococcus, not gonococcus.
She had a sore throat! Drop your trousers, bend over and I'll give
you a jab that'll fix it."

A few weeks later, another fact of life in Bangkok hit me. It was
August, the middle of the rainy season, and it rained heavily
every day. Floods were virtually an annual occurrence, but a
successful mayoral candidate in the run-up to the local Bangkok
Metropolitan Authority elections had promised that that year, if he
was appointed, floods in Bangkok would be a thing of the past. Now
that he had the chain of office around his neck, everyone waited to
see what would happen once the rains moved into top gear.

The night before the big inundation of 1983, I had been invited
to a party at the home of one of my competitors. About 2 a.m., I
looked out of the window at the street behind the apartment block
where all the cars were parked, to find – no cars! My first thought
was that they had all been towed away, but then the reflection of
a streetlight revealed that all the cars were in fact under water. It
takes no effort to imagine the state of the streets once the waters
had receded, the stench emanating from the drains and the smell
that came from my car for weeks, even after I'd had it steam
cleaned. Quite disgusting.

The next day, some opponents of the new mayor arranged for
boat races to be held in the floods along the length of Sukhumvit
Road – the most important shopping highway in the city – just to
ram home the point that political promises were not worth much.
The whole episode reminded me of the story of the English King
Canute, who was told that, given his limitless power, he could even
command the tide to go back if he wished. Keen to put his fawning
courtiers in their place, he had his throne moved to the beach so
he could command the sea to obey him. His failure to convince the
tide to recede succeeded in embarrassing his courtiers – and in
him getting his feet wet. The new mayor certainly got his feet wet,
metaphorically speaking, if not in reality. His 'reign' didn't last long.

One of my clients, a Danish trading company, was very embarrassed by the same flood – much to the annoyance of the Bangkok Metropolitan Authority and to the amusement of the expat community. Flood waters had entered its warehouses, causing millions of baht of damage. By itself this caused no particular concerns for the company because there was considerable insurance cover against such losses, but steps were immediately taken to avoid related problems. One of his major lines was an international brand of sanitary towel. After a small flood a few years before, some enterprising employees had taken wet products which the company considered worthless, dried them out and then sold them on street stalls.

To avoid a recurrence this time, the soaking boxes of sanitary towels were bulldozed into the yard in front of the warehouse, and the MD's driver tasked with buying paint to spray over the mound, making the towels unsaleable. Unfortunately, the driver had chosen to buy red paint. That night there was further rain and the floods returned, washing the painted towels out of the yard, and distributing them for many miles around the warehouse on hedges and barbed wire. Most unfortunate!

After a while I found Thailand to be less 'foreign' and, having accepted what initially appeared as very odd, Bangkok became home. But even then, local oddities never failed to surprise me from time to time.

Citizens with a private phone needed a pin number in order to direct-dial international numbers, because the introduction of direct dialling found many Thais running up bills for foreign calls they couldn't afford. After moving apartments, I realised I would need a new pin. It was late in the evening so, as I had no replacement pin number for my new home, all the switchboard operator could suggest was that I drive down to the 24-hour international telephone exchange in the centre of Town to call New York from there. Parking outside, I noticed that there were no lights on in the exchange, so I asked a guard if I had come to the right place.

"Yes, this is the 24-hour exchange, but it closes at 10 p.m."

Clearly, he saw no anomaly in what he had just said.

93

During the 1970s and 1980s, military coups occurred regularly too, though not every year like the floods. They were a peculiarly Thai phenomenon. Usually no shots were ever fired. It seemed as though two opposing army factions would leave their barracks and face off against each other in the streets of the major cities. No one seemed to know quite what happened next– maybe there was some sort of head count with the larger faction winning – but thereafter the vanquished generals would fly off into exile for a few years. Coups caused some disruption to normal life, but, like most Bangkok residents, my staff shrugged them off as "just one of those things" and carried on.

Traditionally, Thai governments have survived through this amazing sense of pragmatism. For instance, whenever the country had been in danger from foreign invasions, be they from French boats sailing up the Chao Phraya river to Bangkok or Japanese armies arriving in the capital over land during the Second World War, the Thais welcomed the would-be invader. No takeover (as such) has occurred in modern times. It is very hard to attack when you're being garlanded with flowers by Thai maidens.

With the same sense of pragmatism, during the 1980s the army found that military watch towers in the jungle close to the Malaysian border were regularly left unmanned. Soldiers were simply going absent without leave. The government's solution? Provide each tower with an inflatable plastic sex doll to keep bored soldiers occupied. I don't know how well the soldiers would have repelled insurgents with their trousers down, but the incidence of absenteeism fell sharply.

In the same part of the country, communist terrorists were causing trouble. Send in the army? Try a re-education programme? No. The government simply offered a piece of land to any rebel who came out of the jungle, and who (with government incentives) built a home on their own plot of land given to them at no cost. It is hard to be a communist when you're a landowner. This way everyone wins, with no bloodshed. Perhaps Western governments could learn something from the Thai approach to conflict management.

All expatriates in Asia find local attempts to communicate in English amusing when not only is the message incorrect, but the error is entertaining in itself. I have always felt we shouldn't poke fun at Asians' attempts to speak our language, seeing that so few of us bother to try to speak theirs. But some examples from Thailand really are worth sharing.

The leading brand of women's underwear in the kingdom is called 'Fanny' – yes, really. (Try Googling: "Fanny Underwear Thailand"). Not only would we see this as a bizarre choice of name, but it also leads to some unfortunate usages. The company's head office in Bangkok has a shop displaying its wares in large windows at street level. A prominent sign across the front of the building announces "Fanny Showroom". The name is of course appropriate when written in Thai characters and read by a Thai who doesn't speak English, but the transliteration into English could usefully have been a little looser – perhaps "Finny" or "Fenny". (I don't think "Funny Underwear" would have been much of an improvement.)

Maybe the name has some regional significance, because in Vietnam 'Fanny' is a premium ice-cream brand. Moreover, a leading brand of toilet tissue in the region is called 'Kiss Me'.

A tourist shop next to the five-star Dusit Thani Hotel called itself 'The Dear Shop'. The owner was evidently aware of the affectionate use of the word "dear", without fully appreciating its second connotation – particularly unfortunate where retailing is concerned.

On a ferry on the Thai coast, passengers are encouraged to warn the crew should there be a fire by breaking the glass on a fire alarm. The message above the glass reads: "In Case of Fire, Break Wind".

In the centre of Bangkok is 'New Road'. Nothing unusual in that, except it's the oldest road in Bangkok. The city is often called 'The Venice of the East' because canals criss-cross much of the riverside conurbation. A few hundred years ago, the only means of commuting was by boat. The French and British ambassadors found this most inconvenient, so they jointly paid for the canal running between their two embassies to be filled in and a road constructed on it. New Road was the result.

My favourite was a sign on the door of my hotel bedroom in Chiang Mai in the north of the country. It commanded solemnly: "Guests must not up anyone in their room." I felt like informing the management I had never "upped" anyone in a hotel room, and wasn't about to start!

Some cultural differences can be made to work to your advantage, as a friend from the British Club discovered. Barry was a Scot who worked for the United Nations at their regional headquarters in Bangkok. After three years he met a Thai girl, Yuwadi, and just six months after that they got married. Their lives together were happy, and that happiness was increased still further a few months later, when she announced her pregnancy.

Baby George was born without difficulty and six months later the proud parents reserved flights to take their new son to Scotland to meet his grandparents. An interview was booked at the British Embassy to apply for a passport for their son. The interviewer regretted that a passport would take many months because Barry hadn't informed the embassy of his residence in Thailand, his marriage to a foreigner, the pregnancy, or the birth of a child. In fact, he had even waited until George was a few months old before making an application. How was the embassy to know whether they were really married, or the young boy really theirs, etc., etc., without significant checking?

It was suggested that, as they had already booked a flight, they should apply for a Thai passport for George first, as this would be more likely to be approved in time. So that is what they did. Unfortunately, the Thai Passport Office also refused to give George a passport because his mother, having married a foreigner, was in a legal sense now no longer considered 100% Thai.

What could they do? Easy – at least in Thailand. They got divorced.

The paperwork was simple and their divorce confirmed forty-eight hours later. Now, as a single woman, Yuwadi could apply for a passport for George – an application that the Thai government immediately approved. The following day they were re-married, and three weeks after that they flew to Heathrow and then on to Scotland for their holiday.

Two years later, Barry left the UN and took a job with a Bangkok-based trading company. The couple had decided to make Bangkok their permanent home and began looking for a house to buy. Having found one, they were hit by another bureaucratic problem. Foreigners can buy apartments, but not landed properties. Barry couldn't buy a house and neither could Yuwadi because – you guessed it – she was no longer considered 100% Thai.

So they got divorced a second time. Once single, Yuwadi bought the house. They waited a few days for the legal paperwork to be completed and then married for a third time. (I wonder how many times they have been divorced now, seeing they were first married some forty years ago?)

The workings of Thai law never ceased to amuse me. In the early 1980s Bangkok had a fleet of buses that I joked were 'magic'. As they pulled away from the curb they would 'disappear' in seconds, as if by magic, behind an impenetrable cloud of filthy diesel fumes. A new mayor decided this was unacceptable and a transportation commission subcommittee was set up to look into purchasing a new fleet of less polluting vehicles.

In time, the committee was further divided into two, one half going to the bus manufacturer Tata in Japan, while the other went to British Leyland in the UK to look into the idea of having double-decker buses on Bangkok streets. One month later the two sub-groups met for a joint session... only to find that *they had both signed uncancellable contracts* for a completely new fleet. What to do?

It was decided that the uncancellable English contract would be cancelled. The British legal objections were overruled by the local courts in Bangkok. The reason given was, and I quote: "The purchase of double-decker buses would allow unruly elements to ride on the upper deck and spit down on the bald heads of monks."

Mind you, the law can be an ass in other countries too. However, sometimes judges cut through all the complexities of the legal arguments and offer clear, simple logic, which none of the barristers on either side had even considered.

In the UK, while I was working on the Jaffa Cake account, the government decided to change the tax code. Food would remain free of VAT, but snacks would attract the standard VAT rate. My client decided that Jaffa Cakes were, as the name suggested, a cake and therefore a food, thus VAT free. The Inland Revenue decided they were biscuits and took United Biscuits to court to have the brand re-designated a biscuit/snack, and to demand back taxes.

So is a Jaffa Cake a biscuit or a cake? After many hours of conflicting legal arguments, the judge decided on the simplest of logical tests to settle the matter. Two months later (the law doesn't rush important matters such as this), it was decided that Jaffa Cakes were indeed cakes. His Honour's rationale was simply that if a biscuit is left out in the open air it goes soft, but if a cake is left out it goes hard. His "scientific" experiment of leaving some Jaffa Cakes out on his office desk created a dry, inedible product. So Jaffa Cakes were indeed designated as cakes.

Back in Thailand, I received a telexed request from the Sydney office asking for my help in their attempt to win a new client that manufactured lawnmowers and was interested in exporting to Asia. Keen to demonstrate that our agency had an excellent network of offices across the Asian region ready to help, they contacted me and the other Asian MDs.

The telex simply asked: "What can you tell us about the Thai domestic lawnmower market?"

I'm afraid my reply wasn't as helpful as they had hoped. It asked simply: "What's a lawn?"

Other briefs were equally challenging. You might find it strange if I talk about the morality of the advertising industry, especially in a country like Thailand, where official controls on the veracity of what is claimed in ads are "relaxed". However, there were times when I have felt uncomfortable with the claims we were being asked to make in our commercials. For instance, I have never advertised cigarettes in any country.

As another example, having won the business of a major Japanese white goods manufacturer, we were asked to make a TV commercial for its branded washing machines. It seemed nearly

70% of all washing machines sold in Thailand came from this sole manufacturer, but only 25% of them carried the company's brand name. The other 75% were sold under a Thai name or that of a Thai retailer.

Machines carrying the client's lead brand name were approximately a third more expensive than the locally branded ones. When I asked in what way the client's branded machines were superior, I was told they were not. Consumers were simply paying a premium for the famous name. The cheaper versions might have minor cosmetic differences, but their function and reliability were identical. This meant we had to convince housewives to pay 30% more than they would otherwise need to, for no material advantage.

Having determined that the ads would not make any false claims, I accepted the brief. After all, the purpose of all brand advertising is to suggest that branded goods offer the benefit of familiarity, trust and reassurance built up over time. This might not be a physical benefit, but a very real psychological one, nonetheless. Buyers could decide for themselves whether this reassurance was worth a 30% premium.

The resultant TV commercial showed a woman and her children and carried the end slogan: "The clear choice of loving mothers around the world." My conscience felt clear – well, reasonably clear.

Towards the end of my time in the country, there was one difficult conversation I remember above all others. Not a conversation with a client, employee, or global colleague, but one that involved far more effort and caused more personal embarrassment.

I was woken by the telephone beside my bed at my hotel in Phuket during a weekend away. It had been a long evening of beers and local food, and I was deeply asleep when the phone started ringing. The conversation went as follows:

"Mornee!"

"Mornee, I mean... sorry... good morning."

"Djew wan brefass?"

"Yes please, I'd love some breakfast."

"Djew wantoes why?

"Pardon"

"Djew... wan... toes why?"

"I'm really sorry, but I don't understand djew wantoes why."

"DJEW... WAN... TOES WHY?"

"Oh, I get it, you're asking whether I'd like white toast."

"Rye."

"Yes, two slices please."

"Wid botta?"

"Yes please, with botta... I mean butter. On the side please."

"Rye! Djew wan eeks?"

"I'm sorry, I really don't..."

"Eeks. Fri eeks."

"Oh yes, fried eggs please."

"Wi sossis gree?"

"I'm sorry, what is sossis gree?"

"Fri eeks wi SOSSIS GREE."

"Yes, yes... Fried eggs with grilled sausages. Yes, I'd love that."

"Crissybagon?"

"Ah yes, I've got it. You mean crispy bacon?"

"Rye. Why coffee?"

"Yes please. White coffee."

"Thas Room 213. Brefass. Two toes why, wid botta on si. Fri eeks wi sossi gree an crissybagon, coffee why. OK?"

"Very much OK. Thank you."

After that, I fell back into an exhausted sleep until my breakfast arrived.

All good things really do come to an end, but ideally endings, like beginnings, should be planned. With me they never seemed to be. I didn't plan to leave Bangkok after two enjoyable years, but Fate took a hand as usual.

One lunchtime I felt really hungry. It was 12.45, so I headed for somewhere I knew I could get a really good quick lunch, where English would be spoken by all the staff – the Oriental Hotel. As I walked through the lobby, I noticed a European sitting in an easy chair reading the London *Daily Telegraph*. He seemed familiar, but very much my senior. A friend of my father, perhaps?

Complaints from my stomach were louder than the queries from my memory, so I left the man to his news and entered the coffee shop to eat. Twenty five minutes later I re-emerged to find that my mystery man was still there. As I walked towards him, he looked up, smiled and said: "Hey! Hello, it's been a long time."

"Good to see you too. How are things back at home?" My smile hopefully hid my complete ignorance of this man's identity, while he even knew my name. "Come on," I thought. "Give me a clue. Who the hell are you?"

"Life goes on in St James's Square much as before," he said. "You probably know I took over your accounts when you left for Singapore. Well, now I run the international business. Peggy complains she never sees me much anymore, and to be honest I'm getting tired of living out of a suitcase. Don't suppose you have plans to come home any time soon? I'm retiring in about six months and we haven't found anyone to replace me yet. I'd have thought you'd be ideal. You know the clients – or at least most of them – and you must have a good deal of international experience after all this time in Asia. Tell me what you've been up to."

Of course, Claude Raft. So the old bugger had been keeping my seat warm these past eight and a half years, and now he was offering its return. There'd been times I had wondered exactly how I could engineer a return to London. I wasn't sure to what extent my experience in the Mystic East would be in my favour. Would I be seen as someone who'd spent far too long outside the mainstream advertising world to take on a senior role back in Europe?

I took Claude on a tour of my agency, followed by an evening that Peggy would never get to hear about, I'm quite sure.

And I was back in London to toast him at his leaving party at Simpsons in the Strand just thirty-six weeks later. It was good to be home.

Chapter 10

London, 1984–1992

It had taken many rapid adjustments on my part to live and work in Singapore and Bangkok, not to mention Tokyo, Brunei, Chicago and Jakarta, but I found it no easier settling back into London. Most things hadn't really changed that much, they just had to be remembered and re-adjusted to, like supermarket shopping, doing my own cooking and laundry, and re-registering with my old doctor. It was I who had changed.

A few other things really were new. There had been no radio advertising when I left, but now commercial radio stations could be found all over the dial of my little portable set, each one accepting advertising. And there were new TV stations that clients wanted to advertise on as well. But in my new exalted role as Senior Vice President (International), I had to adjust to commercial life not only in the UK, but in so many countries around the world I hadn't even visited up to that point. How should the new United Airways advertising theme be adjusted to make it relevant in Argentina, Albania or maybe Australia?

I knew better than most that foreign countries were often very... well ... foreign. A tourist staying in an international hotel probably will not notice the nuances of cultural difference in a country, but an advertising agency must be fully aware of them, in order to make sure ads sound "local" and relevant to the country's consumers.

I didn't want to make a mistake similar to the one made by the manufacturers of More cigarettes. This (then) new American cigarette - the first to be aimed specifically at female smokers - was launched in Europe without someone pointing out that the French word for 'death' was *mort* (pronounced 'more'). Not the best name for a cigarette when cigarette-related deaths were becoming a major health issue.

Our client British Airways had a slogan that posed no problems when translated into various foreign languages, and was used for decades :- "The World's Favourite Airline". At first sight it seemed to me to be an impossible over-exaggeration. How could BA support such a claim when they were so much smaller than many other airlines? Surely they hadn't researched travellers opinions in every country to which they flew.

No, it was far simpler than that, but equally defendable. BA flew predominately short-haul flights, so whilst they weren't the biggest airline by a wide margin, more people made a decision to fly BA more often than any other airline. In this way a BA flight from London to Paris counted as one flying decision by each passenger on board, whilst a United Airlines passenger flying from Los Angeles to Paris would be one flight decision too. So in this way it could be claimed that more passengers made a decision to fly with BA than with any other airline. Therefore BA must be the world's favourite airline!

Most of my time in the new job was spent in Europe, which made my travelling schedule easier and minimised the need to take long-haul flights. However, even within one culturally mature continent there were consumer differences to adjust to.

For instance, one of my clients decided to sponsor the Barcelona Olympic Games. In competition with three other agencies, we were charged with recommending a TV campaign to run in Europe to announce and generate benefit from this sponsorship.

Our idea was simple. My presentation to the client's European representatives centred around the fact that, as an official sponsor, they had access to any film footage of previous games owned by the

Olympic Committee – film that could be used free of charge. I could immediately see that the idea of essentially "free" commercial production had great appeal to the assembled clients, particularly as the Olympic commercials would have a life of just a few weeks.

Of course, they asked me how we would make use of this footage in the creation of TV commercials. I explained that at times things go wrong at the Olympic Games, many examples of which are amusing. Like the poor pole vault athlete whose pole snaps just as he is about to reach maximum altitude, or the marathon runner who trips and splashes headfirst into a water-filled ditch. Humour crosses borders and is universally appreciated – isn't it?

At this point the French client, known for his wicked sense of humour, asked in apparent innocence: "Do you plan to show these commercials everywhere in Europe?"

"Yes."

"Surely not in Germany!"

There was much laughter among the assembled national client representatives, until their German colleague jumped to his feet with anger written all over his face. "Joking about ze German sense of humour IS NO LAUGHING MATTER!"

This brought the house down and the angry German stomped out. Our recommendations were approved after a mere five minutes of further discussion and we won the pitch, but the incident showed that not only did consumer attitudes vary across the countries of the continent, clients' attitudes differed too.

There were other things I had to adjust to as I travelled around Europe. One I referred to as "stomach lag". There was no jet lag for me to suffer from because of the short journeys involved, but "stomach lag" could be just as debilitating.

For instance, I regularly caught the Heathrow to Hamburg British Airways flight that left at 07.10, requiring me to get out of bed at 04.10. After dressing quickly, I would eat a hastily prepared bowl of cereal and drink a cup of coffee. In the airport lounge I would eat a pastry or two and a second cup of coffee. On the plane, those of us lucky enough to be in Business Class would be served a light breakfast, so when I found myself on German soil I was well fuelled for the day.

I would arrive at the Hamburg office around 11 a.m., or 10 a.m. according to my stomach, which did not appreciate time differences. After an hour there would be a break for lunch - Germans generally taking their midday meal early, by my standards at least. This was a meal I would have happily missed, but, ever polite, I felt obliged to join them, and of course enjoyed every mouthful.

After a mid-afternoon flight to Madrid, I would find myself unpacking in my hotel with little to do before dining with my Spanish colleagues. I quickly found out that the Spanish eat their evening meal very late, so my stomach had to bridge the time gap between my German lunch at noon and my Spanish dinner at 9p.m. or 10p.m.

One other practical matter caught me out during my first few weeks of travelling around Europe. With so many countries to visit, I tried to time my meetings and flights to provide maximum efficiency. However, efficiency isn't everything.

I soon realised that if I didn't occasionally spend two nights in an hotel I wouldn't be able to get my laundry done, so I'd end up back in the UK with a suitcase full of dirty clothes that needed to be washed, dried and ironed before I could travel with them again.

While it is important to take account of national differences, some "truths" are true in every market. One of my visits to Oslo reminded me of a very relevant industry saying:

Keep it simple: Keep it stupid.

Those of us in the industry must remember that consumers do their best to ignore ads, particularly if they pop up in the middle of their favourite TV programme. Most would deny being influenced by advertising at all, and sadly millions of pounds worth of advertising really does go unnoticed as consumers flick through newspapers or drive past billboards. After all, they don't *need* advertising in the way we need them to notice our ads. Then, having noticed the ad they needed to be convinced by it, and finally needed to buy our clients' brands.

For instance, the Oslo office had been briefed by the city council to promote its library service. It wanted a TV commercial that listed all the libraries, with their addresses, telephone numbers, opening hours and any special book collections they might have. Correctly, the agency declined the brief. It argued that keen book readers would know where their local library was, or could easily find out, while others wouldn't take in all the detail of addresses, times, and dates – especially not from a thirty-second TV commercial. Folk do not watch TV with a pad and pencil at their elbow so they can note down the contents of commercials.

In its place, the agency suggested that the local government's objective should be simply to encourage more people to read more books. Why else have libraries? If people wanted to read books (without buying them all), they would find their local library and its opening times. All the client should set out to do was suggest an eye-catching reason why people should read more books.

This was eventually agreed, and an award-winning TV commercial was made. The single-shot commercial opened on a scene of two men sitting side by side on a train: the one nearest the window reading a magazine, the other a hard-back book. After a couple of seconds there is the buzzing sound of a fly. The man with the magazine frantically tries and fails to swat the fly with his rolled up magazine, while the book reader is unmoved. Eventually the book reader snaps his book shut. The buzzing stops. He re-opens the book and flicks the dead fly away. No words, just one continuous shot.

Over the last few seconds, the following slogan appeared on screen: "It pays to read books."

The client was thrilled to have won an advertising award. More importantly, after all the press coverage, the footfall in libraries increased. Research also showed that the humour used had reduced the boring image that is enjoyed by libraries worldwide. In every sense, the Oslo libraries became more approachable and more heavily used.

Chapter 11

Russia and Eastern Europe

In the mid-1980s the Soviet Union still directly or indirectly controlled a large swathe of Eastern Europe. When looking at the potential for doing business with countries that were still communist, my clients in the West fell into two distinct groups:

- Those who thought these countries were in the "too difficult" category and should not be viewed as viable markets until they saw the good sense of becoming more capitalist in outlook.
- Those who realised that some form of normalisation between East and West was sure to occur: it was only a matter of time. The Western companies who were there first would enjoy a massive advantage. Tens of millions of would-be shoppers in Eastern Europe were longing for Western consumer goods to become available.

This second group of clients took up much of my time. Clearly, when they did open an office in Sofia or Warsaw they would need an advertising agency. We would gain their business if we were one step ahead of our competitors, by being already on the ground and conversant with the practicalities of getting advertising produced and distributed locally.

My job was to make it happen.

I recommended that we start by finding a suitable joint venture partner in each country, because at that time most Eastern European countries were not ready to allow foreign companies to operate foreign-owned advertising agencies on their soil. Moreover, how else could I go about setting up and running a local office without any local knowledge? Especially since I didn't speak any of the Eastern European languages.

This logic was inescapable, but unfortunately it posed a second question for me: How do you find a suitably experienced joint venture partner when local advertising agencies (as we knew them) didn't exist yet?

I decided to start with the country that would offer the greatest potential, though probably the greatest start-up difficulties too.

I began my search for a Russian joint venture partner at the Institute of Directors, which was just a short walk from my office in St James Square. There, an old contact of mine agreed to arrange a meeting for me with an International Trade Development Officer at the Foreign Office.

Two days later, I was being ushered into an office in Whitehall, where two balding men rose from their chairs to greet me. The taller of the two introduced himself as the Trade Development Officer I had come to see. He explained that his colleague was an ex-commercial attaché from the British embassy in Moscow. As this second man came towards me with his hand outstretched, I almost expected him to say in a soft Scots drawl: "The name's Bond James Bond." (I have no idea what a real spy looks like, but my imagination immediately suggested this was his true profession.)

He began with an introduction to doing business in the Soviet Union that shocked me; I even began to wonder whether this commercial challenge was going to be one step too far for my clients, my agency and, most importantly, for me too.

As though keen to discourage me, he started with: "First things first. The Soviet Union is in a very fragile state – not because of anything we or the Americans might be doing, but because of major fissures in the Russian body politic. I don't know whether the Soviet Union will collapse this year, next year or the year after, but collapse it will, and you are just going to have to hope that you are not around when it does. It won't be pretty. Just in case it should happen when you are over there, these are the precautions you should take.

"Firstly, always have a money belt under your shirt with at least $5,000 in it. This is not to be spent in Russia unless the worst happens, so your usual expenses would be extra. The $5,000 is to get you out of Russia and into Finland. You would probably be hitch-hiking, but wherever you are in Russia, be sure you have worked out the route you would need to take to get to Helsinki, if push comes to shove. Do not change the dollars into roubles. They are just about worthless: nobody will want them.

"You should also take with you at least four hundred Marlboro cigarettes. They are an unofficial currency that will get you taxi rides, and are likely even to silence an inquisitive border guard. You'll just have to guess what the going rate is for whatever favour you require, but twenty Marlboros has been enough to get me a taxi ride from one side of Moscow to the other.

"Next, go to the Hospital for Tropical Diseases in Tottenham Court Road here in London. I know you aren't going to the tropics, but they'll check you have all the travel jabs you need. Also ask them for one of their Extreme Travel Kits, which has everything you could need, including morphine, broad-spectrum antibiotics and two syringes. In Russia you have to work on the assumption that even if you find a doctor when you want one, they won't have the medication you require, and it is reassuring to know the needle being pushed into your arm is yours, and therefore clean.

"Finally, in preparation for your stay, take with you a good stock of chocolate and other snacks, because outside your Intourist hotel, food may well be scarce. In Russia you can really claim that 'A Mars a day helps you work, rest and play'.

"Once you've arrived," he continued, "it is important that you assume that everything you say will be heard by the authorities. Political, or in any sense critical, *thoughts* are pretty safe, just don't express them to anybody. At least one of your staff will be reporting your every move. I believe you are not married, which is going to be helpful, because it will be harder to blackmail you over any... indiscretions you may become guilty of. Don't even think of going behind the Iron Curtain if you fancy boys and have any problems controlling yourself. However, beware of all types of honeytrap. They can be... well... sticky."

The prospect of being in Russia 'when the balloon goes up' was something I could imagine because, back in 1968 during a holiday in Eastern Europe, I had experienced something similar. With some old school friends we were visiting Prague, staying in a loft room in a down-at-heel hotel. As we did every night, we ate at a small restaurant nearby and consumed rather more local beer and wine than a very young adult should. I collapsed into bed around midnight, still fully dressed, and fell immediately into a very deep sleep.

Some hours later, a very loud grinding, screeching noise filled my head. I placed my hands over my ears to try to block it out and stop my brain from exploding. My first thought was I must have drunk even more than usual to create such a reaction in my head. Unable to reduce the noise or go back to sleep, I staggered upright and went to the window for some fresh air. Pushing the curtains aside, I was horrified to see a column of Russian tanks heading towards the centre of the city.

This was very scary, though I can remember the sense of relief when I realised that the noises were from tank tracks rolling over cobbled streets, rather than the result of alcohol attacking my brain cells. I was witnessing Day 1 of the end of the 'Prague Spring'.

Back at the Foreign Office, I took a large gulp of water from the glass in front of me. Next, the trade development officer started his part of the briefing.

"You've mentioned you will want to find a joint venture partner. Obviously, you would like to find a company that can write ads and get them into the press and on to TV in Russia. The only folk with creative skills who know how to get things published are likely to be working for the government on propaganda exercises. In other words, what the government wants to communicate, rather than what you might want consumers to hear. I suggest they aren't what you need. They'd hardly be marketing orientated, would they? You'd be better off 'growing your own'.

"Having warned you off certain government departments, you must realise that pretty much everyone works for the government, in one form or another. As a first priority, I suggest you look for an organisation with political influence because, as the first foreign advertising joint venture, you will only be allowed to operate if those at the top of government decide that you may.

"I have a suggestion for a partner – The Promstroybank," he advised. "Obviously, it is government owned, but it differs from the other major banks in that all Russian companies wishing to trade overseas must do so through an account with them. In the future, some of these companies are bound to want to use you to help with their exports and setting up operations overseas. You could presumably get a list of such clients from the bank on demand. I bet also that the bank will want to spread its wings overseas as soon as it is allowed to. Presumably, it will need commercial contacts in London, New York, Zurich, Singapore and Hong Kong, at the very least – contacts your agency can supply, I'm sure."

An hour later, I left the briefing pretty much in a daze. I had been given so much to think about before I could brief the international board and begin our move into these totally uncharted waters.

Quite understandably, I felt nervous as I boarded the flight from Heathrow to Moscow on my first visit. On arrival, I found a quiet airport with none of the visible tight security I had expected. The immigration officer was polite and almost friendly, and getting a taxi to my hotel was easy. I felt almost disappointed.

I'd had a very different experience of communist-style security some months earlier. My boss, the President of the Board all the way from New York, had decided to visit various European offices. I'd planned to spend two days with him in Hamburg, but after one day we had finished our agenda and he had seen enough.

"Have you ever been to Berlin?" he asked.

"No, I haven't. There hasn't been any business reason to go there, but I've always wanted to."

"Well, as we have a day in hand, why don't I see if our tickets can be changed so we go back to London via Berlin? It's only a short hop from here. I'll ask Gerhardt if he can get someone to make enquiries for us."

After lunch, we headed for the airport with our new tickets. The check-in desk for flights to Berlin was in a separate part of the terminal from all the others. Security was strict and started with us both having to fill in detailed departure/arrival cards. I completed mine and handed it to the uniformed security guard.

"You say here that you are 1.9 metres tall. That is impossible. Please walk this way." He strutted off self-importantly.

I immediately thought of the old music hall joke "I can't walk that way – my trousers are far too tight", but I wasn't brave (or stupid) enough for that. Not being used to metres and centimetres, I had had to guess my height, and had obviously got it wrong. I was led to a windowless room and told to strip. They checked my clothes carefully – heaven knows what they thought they might find – and then looked over my naked body. My attaché case was minutely studied as well.

Apparently satisfied, they allowed me to dress and led me back to the check-in desk. The boss asked me what had happened. When I told him, he fell about laughing.

At this point, the same guard came over and demanded that the president go with him to the same room in order to search him too. When the boss returned, somewhat red-faced, I had to resist the temptation to giggle, not knowing what the guard would want to check this time if I did. I also sensed that laughter might not be too good for my career.

Berlin was fascinating, with visits to Check Point Charlie and all the other "must-see" places. The embarrassment at the airport was worthwhile.

Back in Moscow, once the taxi had reached the outskirts of the city, I could see little more than boring grey concrete residential block after boring grey concrete residential block. There was no evidence of design, decoration, or any attempt to differentiate one block from another. No visible parks or recreation areas either. The scene was very drab, a word that, perhaps a little unfairly, could be used to describe the pedestrians on the footpaths, all wearing colourless and shapeless garments designed, one would think, simply to keep out the cold rather than express a personality or attract the opposite sex.

My Intourist hotel was unremarkable and was just like many others that boasted four stars anywhere else in the world. Similarly, my room was pretty standard. As I unpacked, I was tempted to see if I could find any microphones or cameras, but thought it unwise.

Within minutes of my arrival, the phone rang. A woman's voice asked if there were any 'services' I required. I declined her offer.

That night my bedside phone rang roughly every hour with similar offerings. No matter how strongly I worded my lack of interest in what I guessed was being offered, the very persistent woman clearly did not like to take 'No' for an answer.

In the morning, having been told that each floor had a security guard stationed close to the lift, my first act after dressing was to find him and explain my great frustration at the phone calls. I passed him a packet of twenty Marlboros with the hope that the calls would cease. I was very relieved when they did for the rest of my stay.

Breakfast each morning was a revelation. The food on offer in the buffet varied daily. Quite simply, even an Intourist government-run hotel had difficulty buying basics like eggs and bacon.

While the Promstroybank building was large and impressive, I was ushered in through a less than impressive side door to an office with six desks. Two Russians were there to greet me: Nikolai, who was to become my general manager, and Mikhail. Both spoke excellent English and said they'd been transferred from Promstroybank to the joint venture.

Following a letter to the bank from my agency's president in New York, making an initial proposal of a joint venture, it appeared that the bank had immediately decided that a joint venture would be an excellent idea, and had already received approval from the powers that be. So that was that. It seemed we were ready to begin, and I had apparently employed my first two staff members, even if there was no joint venture contract or even a formal letter of intent to underpin it all.

Slightly taken aback, I asked for coffee and spent the next few hours finding out all I could about my two new employees – this taking the place of the normal interview process. All very strange, but it simplified my life no end not to have to search for suitably qualified staff (whatever "suitably qualified" would mean in this case) and interview them, while simultaneously negotiating contract terms with my new partners.

Over the next few days, I briefed the two men about our international agency structure and history, and then told them as much as I thought they'd be able to immediately absorb about marketing theory and the role of advertising agencies. They found it hard to believe that large manufacturers of consumer goods, headed by really important and very well-paid CEOs, based their decision making on the opinions of their customers! The thought that people of no consequence could dictate to top industrialists was quite beyond them. After all, in Russia people in a ministry office somewhere would decide what was to be manufactured, to what design, and in what quantities. The role of customers was to buy, consume and be grateful.

As always in such circumstances, in this teaching process I was learning from them too. There were things about life in Russia I found hard to understand. For instance, why did most pedestrians – men and women – walk the streets carrying an empty shopping bag? It was explained that the supply of things to buy was never sufficient and, while they didn't believe anyone actually starved, there was always the hope that a shop would be in the process of being re-stocked just as you walked past. If so, a queue would form immediately, with shoppers hoping to get to the front of the line before everything had sold out again. It didn't really matter what was being sold, because undesired items could be bartered with neighbours for whatever was needed. I had experienced the sad effects of money shortages in many countries, although never before a country where the population had sufficient money but a shortage of things to spend it on.

Other problems were explained to me too. For instance, potatoes – the staple carbohydrate in any Russian diet – were sold in sealed brown paper bags. Once the bag was opened at home, the purchaser would be able to see what percentage were actually edible; some would be almost certainly brown, mushy, and bad. This made me think immediately of my UK client that had recently launched Yeoman Mashed Potato. While instant mash might not be every Russian's ideal form of the vegetable, they would at least know that 100% of every pack would be edible.

In the coming days I got to know my two new colleagues really quite well. I had a strong feeling that Nikolai was KGB, or at least ex-KGB. His mother was a retired schoolteacher who I met during my second week in Moscow. Initially she had been reluctant to meet me after decades of propaganda about the evil people in the West who were hell bent on destroying Mother Russia. But eventually she relented, though we got little further than a smile and a handshake, because she spoke no English.

My breakthrough with her happened during my third visit to Moscow, when I brought her a DVD of some *Mr Bean* episodes. It seemed like a good idea because they were funny, they showed life in the West and no foreign words were spoken, just grunts and squeaks. She loved them and looked forward to my visits so she could continue to follow Mr Bean's adventures. Maybe we weren't all bad in the West after all. Nevertheless, she continued to refuse to meet the agency's American president.

Mikhail was a pleasure to talk to. A father of two, he openly hoped that communism would soon come to an end, because he felt sure he had the entrepreneurial flair that eventually would make him rich.

One morning he announced that he had taken his wife for an anniversary dinner the previous evening. When I asked where he had taken her, he proudly showed me a McDonald's box he had kept as a souvenir. I should explain that the first McDonald's outlet in Moscow had only opened a month or two before and was seen as the "coolest" place to eat. Queues often stretched around the block for a Big Mac and fries.

Nikolai was a man who could get things done – one reason I felt sure he was ex-KGB. Russians we came into contact with seemed to be wary of him and seldom disagreed with any request he might have. Mikhail was the "thinker" of the two, a quieter man who listened and considered before acting. They made a great team.

By my second visit to Moscow, we had gained a secretary/ phone answerer/general assistant called Anna, but we had lost our office; or rather, our office had been moved to another part of the building. No reason was given, though Mikhail later whispered to me during a vodka-filled night out that the authorities were concerned that immediately under the floor of the old office were important communications cables that led directly to the Kremlin, so "the capitalist" would have to be accommodated somewhere safer.

It amused me to wonder what risk there might be of me digging up the floor during daylight hours to mess with these cables in an office occupied by four people, three of whom were Russian. Maybe "better safe than sorry" was the KGB motto.

I did what I could to look after my team, to lessen some of the obvious hardships they faced simply by living in Russia. Some items that were unavailable in the local shops were easy to bring with me on my visits. Although they cost very little, they were very much appreciated. For instance, in Moscow it was almost impossible to buy simple first aid necessities such as adhesive dressings, disinfectants, aspirins and all the other pills, creams, lotions and potions every Western home has in its bathroom cabinet. I bought a complete set for each of my employees and found them very gratefully received.

More seriously, Mikhail – a diabetic – stepped on a rusty nail during my third visit and developed a septic foot. Local hospitals could not help him because of the effect his diabetic condition had on the healing process, plus the general lack of availability of most forms of antibiotics. It became clear that within weeks he could lose his foot, leg or even his life. I was able to get him to a private clinic in London that solved the problem in a matter of days. In the clinic I was amused to see him in one of a floor of rooms filled with foreign patients because the ward sister said everyone wanted to have a peek at "the Russian" rather than any of the other of her foreign "guests", as though he might have had two heads or something else which would have marked him out as different.

In return my new Russian staff looked after me too, making sure I didn't make too many faux pas. I learned that Nikolai's translations of my words to the bank's senior officers would sometimes be "massaged" to make them more acceptable. We soon became a tightly knit and efficiently functioning team, and got down to some serious work.

My chocolate client in London decided to prepare the ground for the eventual launch in Russia of its lead product, M&Ms,. At that point it hadn't been worked out how the brand would be imported and distributed, but we were asked to pave the way with PR activity that would raise general consumer awareness. The primary target would be children and their parents.

We recommended simply importing a truckload of product plus some assorted promotional items, such as M&Ms stickers and toys. We would get them distributed in the greater Moscow area via a series of PR activities. The product would be made in the company's Dutch factory, and trucked overland to Moscow.

Nikolai advised that because what we were proposing was unique in his experience, he felt sure our biggest hurdle would be getting the mixed merchandise through customs at the land border. He asked that each and every box be numbered and clearly labelled with its contents. He would need such a list in advance of the truck's arrival, so that he could 'discuss matters' with the customs officers. He would go to the border to have what he called 'a friendly discussion' with them, made more friendly by 'sharing his expenses' with them, and promising that a box or two of chocolates would be given to each of the officers' children as a sign of goodwill.

The customs officers agreed that a thorough search of the truck would not be necessary. Instead, they would pick a couple of boxes at random (the boxes of chocolates they would take to their families) and check them. Just to show willing.

In due course the truck arrived. Its rear doors were opened and a box was selected and checked against Nikolai's list: "Box

113: Individual bags of M&Ms". However, once the box was opened it was found to contain M&Ms promotional children's watches. Contraband!

The boxes had clearly been mislabelled, but the mistake allowed the customs officers all the excuse they needed to open each and every box. Nikolai's expenses were stretched to their limit, and customs officers' children would be eating chocolates until they felt very sick indeed.

Eventually, the truck was released and reached Moscow without further incident. Now we had to get the M&Ms into the hands of the city's children. We planned three events.

The first was held in Red Square during a public holiday. Through the bank, permission was granted to erect a small promotional stand in this most revered of locations, but we thought we would be pushing our luck too far to erect it right outside the main government building or Lenin's mausoleum, within sight of the army guard of honour. However, we hoped that via the local press (which had been briefed in advance), possibly local TV and word of mouth, the story would spread quickly. The local CNN office agreed to cover the event too, so we were hopeful the client would get its money's worth in terms of brand awareness.

A spot outside St Basil's Cathedral grounds was selected – still within Red Square, but at what I hoped would be seen as a respectful distance from the really important areas. Quite a stir was created once we began handing out free bags of chocolate and small toys, not simply because children were attracted to what was on offer, but because they and their parents were very suspicious of anything foreigners were giving away free of charge. Why would any organisation – let alone an American one – give stuff away? What was the catch?

The following week we called on a list of orphanages, again to hand out product. While the orphanages selected may not have been typical, I was relieved to see happy, well-behaved, well-dressed children in modern, clean surroundings. At each stop, Mikhail gave a little speech about the new product that would soon be on sale in the shops (we hoped), and then each child was given a sample. Smiles all round.

Finally, we had managed to sponsor an afternoon performance of *Swan Lake* by the Bolshoi Ballet for groups from local schools. Each child was given a bag of M&Ms with a programme for the ballet. The performance was most enjoyable for me to watch, but I was particularly impressed by how well behaved the children were: not a sound from them during the whole performance.

The next day we reviewed our first consumer-oriented operations in Russia. All of us had learned a lot. The main thing was that even before I reported back, the client had seen everything on CNN – and was very pleased.

I quite expected the other Eastern Bloc countries would present similar experiences, but I couldn't have been more wrong. The least "Russia like" was Slovenia, which some months before my visit in 1991 had declared independence from Yugoslavia. I drove to the capital from Vienna in Austria because the main runway at Ljubljana airport had been bombed during the brief Ten-Day War with the other parts of Yugoslavia, which had been aimed at discouraging any break-up of the country.

Driving through the streets of Ljubljana, I was struck by how like Western Europe it seemed. The shops were open and appeared well stocked, and the buildings weren't shapeless concrete blocks. Everything looked "normal" by Western European standards. It would seem the country had never taken communism to heart. It had had close ties with the West through a largely open border with Austria and Italy, and rapidly flourished after its newly announced independence. The people I saw in the streets looked relaxed, well fed, and dressed just like their neighbours in Austria.

Over the coming years, it didn't surprise me that Slovenia became a full member of the European Union in 2004 and NATO the same year (having never been a member of the Warsaw Pact). Similarly, it was the first ex-communist country to join the Eurozone. It was also the first to have a fully operational advertising agency – with a little help from me. Slovenia was ready for the Iron Curtain to fall.

We decided there would be little point in special PR activities here; the clients would simply launch their brands in the usual way once they had achieved distribution through imports directly from Austria. I found a printing company in Ljubljana that agreed to form a joint venture with us, and without any problems we were soon ready for business.

At the other end of the "ready for business" spectrum was Romania. For me it represented everything that was bad about the Eastern Bloc, with few, if any, redeeming features. It seemed the country had accepted all the drabness, lack of colour and shapelessness of the Russian social model with enthusiasm, and added despair, disrepair and hopelessness for its citizens. The ride from the airport to my dreary hotel passed through communist-style blocks of flats that were clearly in need of more than just a coat of paint.

As a stark contrast, the palace that the government had taken over as the residence of the president, Nicolae Ceauşescu, was magnificent. The government "of the proletariat by the proletariat", with equality for all, didn't seem to be the way Communism actually worked here in practice.

As with Slovenia, I had contacted a large printing company to see if it might be interested in being part of a joint venture. A representative, a blonde interpreter named Anna, called for me at my hotel, from where we could walk to the company's office. The meeting was brief because, as far as I was concerned, the MD had no concept of advertising or marketing and had very little to offer. There simply was no meeting of minds at all.

The walk back to my hotel on a cold, dark winter's evening was very scary. Few of the streetlights were working, and all the shops and offices were closed and in darkness. There was no traffic at all and no other pedestrians, just heavily armed soldiers, or police at every junction.

Maybe I was close to hysteria, but I said to Anna, "Of course, if our companies work together you'll have to learn the company dance." Not surprisingly, she looked puzzled and must have thought she'd misheard me. So I grabbed her hand and started skipping along the street. After a few steps she got the idea and we skipped together the rest of the way, laughing like children. I wondered when those streets had last heard laughter. Thank God we weren't stopped... or shot for that matter!

After a few more visits to Eastern Bloc countries, I recommended to interested clients that they concentrate on the easier countries such as Slovenia, and leave countries like Romania and Albania until last. After all, they would only be able to launch their brands in one country at a time, given all the work required to gain reasonable distribution, and they may as well cut their teeth on the easier ones first.

However, Albania did cause me to smile on two counts. Firstly, I had been warned that there was only one hotel for Westerners in the capital, Tirana. I should make sure I insisted on a room on the third floor, because bedrooms on the other floors had no hot water.

Secondly, on arrival at the airport I went to the Bureau de Change to swap my sterling for leks. From a large safe, the cashier brought out thick wads of notes, which I assumed he would use to re-stock his till before serving me. Instead, he passed the lot over the counter. Bizarrely, I walked away with a Sainsbury's plastic carrier bag half full of bank notes.

When my taxi arrived at my hotel, I had no way of working out how much of my newly exchanged leks the driver would expect. The taxi had no meter, and even if it had, I wouldn't have known whether the figures displayed would be in leks, hundreds of leks, thousands or even tens of thousands. I showed him one of the wads of notes and he indicated with his thumb and forefinger the quantity he felt would be appropriate. My ride cost me about 1.5 inches of leks!

Setting up offices in a variety of countries at much the same time – none of which had an existing advertising industry to draw on – was frustrating and time consuming, but I learned an excellent lesson from the managing director of one of the first international hotels to open in Warsaw. He had been horrified by the standard of service he received whilst staying as a guest in local hotels during the completion of his own.

When he began interviewing staff who would come into contact with guests in his new hotel, he would invariably start by asking what relevant experience they had had. If they said they had served customers in a local Polish hotel, he would end the interview, or offer a job behind the scenes. He was certain it was easier to start from scratch and train new recruits 'from the bottom up', rather than trying to undo all the bad attitudes and habits picked up while working in local hotels.

When interviewing, I too looked for what I considered was the right attitude and keenness to learn, rather than searching for employees who might claim to have just the experience I was looking for. I preferred to "grow my own" too.

Chapter 12

The Rest of My World

While I was rushing around Eastern Europe, a good friend of mine was setting up a company in London – but a rather different one. Mary, an account director, had arrived at her desk at the advertising agency J. Walter Thomson in Berkeley Square one morning to be told she was being made redundant. Would she please clear her desk and leave by 11a.m? She had had no warning this could happen, but just before 11a.m she walked out of the building in a bit of a daze, carrying a box full of her possessions.

Mary then did what any good advertising executive would do. She went to the nearest pub to drown her sorrows. An hour or so later, she watched her employed ex-colleagues coming in for a lunchtime sandwich and a pint. When they had all returned to work, she began chatting to the landlord, who clearly was exhausted by the rush.

He explained that while he made much more money from selling sandwiches than drinks, the purchasing of ingredients, and the process of actually making the sandwiches, wrapping them, and displaying them attractively day after day, was more than he and his wife could really manage. Sensing an opportunity, Mary immediately offered to do all the legwork for him. If he would give her an order for the next day, she would have the sandwiches ready and delivered by 11 a.m. for the lunchtime rush.

The next day, she delivered the sandwiches to the great satisfaction of the landlord. His profit margin on each sandwich was lower than before, of course, but he didn't feel as drained when he called "Time!" and watched his last afternoon customers leave. After a few days of success, Mary approached some neighbouring pubs with a similar offer, which they repeatedly accepted with similar keenness.

After just one month, finding herself overly stretched working alone from her flat, Mary signed a lease on a sandwich bar and hired two friends to run it, while she had other part-time staff in the back room each afternoon making sandwiches for her pub rounds. This represented the advantage of enabling her to prepare large quantities of food for human consumption in premises that had been licensed for the purpose, rather than in her apartment, which had not.

And then there were open-topped sandwiches for board lunches for local companies, and even food for simple civil wedding receptions, as well as the purchase of another sandwich bar. Within 18 months she was a millionaire and never looked back. When working under pressure in an advertising agency, one might be forgiven for thinking there was no commercial career worth considering outside advertising agencies, but it would seem there was.

At one point I actually considered joining Mary. When I mentioned this to my mother, she asked, "Surely you wouldn't be happy buttering bread for the rest of your life?"

"Maybe I would if it was my bread I was buttering," I replied. "Why not?"

Tempting as this alternative career was, I stayed at the agency. I kept a packed suitcase in my office just in case an urgent call came (as it did more often than I liked) and for the next few years I spent a lot of my time "hanging in the sky".

While Russia and Eastern Europe took up a lot of my attention, I was also expected to make sure our clients were being well looked after by our agencies elsewhere in the world. My role was essentially to understand why we achieved success with brands in the major markets, so that this knowledge could be shared with our agencies' and clients' overseas offices. Every country required local adaptations of material created elsewhere, but at least they had a starting point of knowledge to work from, and perhaps even existing TV commercials that could be re-voiced for local use without expensive re-editing or re-shooting.

One evening, I arrived at the Hilton Hotel in Vienna, and immediately went to dinner at a restaurant I knew that cooked my type of food. Returning to my room having had two or three glasses of wine with my meal, I decided to postpone my presentation rehearsal until the morning. I am much more of a morning person when it comes to out-of-hours work, so I went to bed early and set my alarm for a dawn wake-up call.

After getting out of bed at 6 a.m., I showered and switched on CNN to run in the background as I dressed. What I saw on screen completely floored me: cruise missiles flying across the screen and exploding into buildings across Baghdad. The Gulf War was the first battle to be watched live on TV, just as it was happening. And I had a 'front row seat'.

I was transfixed by what I was watching and completely forgot my need to rehearse, or even to order breakfast. Later I left for the office feeling very guilty – and just a little hungry. This was an important client presentation and I had not found the time to rehearse it! (I'm pleased to say it went very well: perhaps my lack of practice and a feeling of guilt contributed to my performance?)

A second memorable visit was to Brazil. We had had a small office there for some time servicing the few (largely US) clients who had businesses in the country. However, we decided to undertake a major survey so we could inform other potential clients about what appeal the country might hold for them. Just how poor was the population, and what sort of products could they afford and what would they want to buy? What were the current trends in consumer purchases? What type of products would be likely to have the most appeal?

I spent a week in São Paulo working with the local team trying to understand the data that had been collected. On the one hand, based on reported income levels, the figures suggested that the majority of consumers simply could not afford to buy premium imported products at all. It made me wonder how they survived on such low incomes, though perhaps there was a difference between their reported income and their actual income. How many citizens actually filled in an income tax declaration at all? After all, who likes paying tax? Seeing that virtually all our clients manufactured relatively expensive international brands, the immediate potential of Brazil seemed small, certainly for their more expensive, non-essential lines. However, healthy sales figures on premium-priced consumer items such as Nike sports shoes and large colour TV sets suggested otherwise.

The agency MD felt he knew why the figures on incomes and sales of premium imports didn't appear to match up. He took me on a drive through the favelas - the city's infamous hillside slums. Just like my evening drive through Chicago years before, I was asked not to unlock the car doors under any circumstances until we returned to the office.

"There are about eleven million people living in the favelas, here and in Rio," the MD explained. "The government is always promising to replace the slum buildings, but they don't seem to realise that knocking down shacks is one thing, building suitable alternative accommodation is another. The local government has tried building on cheaper land well outside the centre of the cities, but then the citizens have to commute – which they aren't prepared to do, or maybe can't afford to do. So the occupants simply rebuild the slums exactly where they were before, changing nothing. Either way, we can't ignore the purchasing power of eleven million people living right here in the big cities."

We drove slowly, looking into bars and cafés and through the open doors of many slum dwellings. While the overall impression was one of poverty, many if not most teenagers seemed be wearing expensive branded shoes and clothing, and all the homes we could look into seemed to have a large colour TV.

It was clear that if an item became sufficiently aspirational and made the desired social statement about the owner, a way would be found to acquire it – be it by prioritising the purchase out of wages and savings, or other means. Given the level of average declared wages in the favelas and the lack of the rule of law, it seemed likely that many items had simply "fallen off the back of a lorry", or had been funded by the sale of drugs.

So perhaps imported cornflakes wouldn't sell well in Brazil, but maybe suitably advertised premium liquor brands just might.

Many of my more memorable trips were to countries much nearer home. Memories of my first trip to Dublin still make me smile.

I was picked up at Dublin airport during a week when the European Union's finance ministers were meeting in the city. My driver asked, "Are you here to discuss the Irish economy? It's a disaster, a complete disaster... but not serious!"

It seemed likely I would be making frequent visits to the Dublin office. To save time, I arranged for a particular taxi firm always to meet me at the airport and I became a regular client. On one occasion, my driver showed what a fantastic sense of humour so many Irish have by asking, "Has Mick ever driven you into the city?"

"Mick? I don't think so," I replied.

"Oh, we are very worried about Mick, you know," he continued gravely. "He came in one Monday morning with a black eye, so we asked him what had happened. He said he had been at Mass the previous day, and was sitting in a row immediately behind a beautiful blonde. He told me, "As she got to her feet to sing a hymn, I noticed that unfortunately the hem of her dress had become tucked into the waistband of her knickers at the back. Feeling sorry for her, I reached forward and pulled the skirt out and smoothed it down. Then she just turned around and punched me in the eye.""

I said nothing, and for the next five miles or so there was silence. Then my driver continued: "This week we have become really worried about Mick, because he came into the office on Monday this week with the other eye all black and blue. When we asked what had happened, he explained: 'Well, yesterday I was at Mass as usual, and by chance was sitting behind the very same blonde. Believe it or not, once again the back of her dress was stuck into the waistband of her knickers. Now, the guy next to me pulled the skirt out, but I knew she didn't like that, so I...'"

I've mentioned before my fascination with what market research can tell us about ordinary folks and the way they lead their lives. I remember becoming involved in a major survey of the pet food market in Holland. Most European countries are "wet" markets – that is to say dog owners predominantly feed their pets canned food as their staple diet, adding in biscuits, scraps, and anything else that comes to hand. However, Holland is very much a "dry" market, with pets fed dry kibbles from a bag, plus scraps rather than "wet" meat in gravy from a can.

As a consequence we wanted to learn whether the Dutch treated their animals differently, or whether they maybe had a different type of relationship with their pets. Was the bond between the animal owner and its pet unique in Holland? The research suggested that the pets and their owners were, in the main, just like animals and pet lovers in every other country.

Around the world, cat owners are very different from dog owners in many ways, though of course, some households boast cats and dogs. Cat owners live with a certain amount of tension in their lives. They are perpetually concerned that their cat will transfer their affections to another household if offered food they prefer. Cats can "disappear" for a number of days. Their human carer panics about these absences, but usually the pet simply strolls back into the house once they are ready to do so, as if they had never been away. Cats clearly believe they are superior to humans.

Cats often accept affection and strokes, but tend to give the impression that they are doing so to please their human, rather than because they are enjoying the attention. At any point they can simply get up and walk off. It seems incontestable that if cats could speak they would talk with some distain about 'the human they own'. Cat owners accept that they cannot control their animal even if they legally own them. In a very real sense, their cat controls them.

Not so dog owners. They treat their pet in the same way they would treat a child. They feel responsible for their animal in the same way they would be responsible for the bringing up of their child : responsible for feeding it, collecting any droppings, making sure it behaves when on the lead, and obeys when off the lead. They would feel mortified if, in the presence of other dog owners in a public space, their dog did not respond immediately when called.

Specifically, owners of small dogs treat them as they would a human toddler, carrying them in their arms, or perhaps a shoulder bag or even a bicycle basket. The words used when talking to their pet reflects this parent–toddler relationship too.

Medium sized dogs have a mother/junior school child relationship, whilst large dogs are spoken to as though they were teenagers. Unlike cats, dogs know their place in the family. They would not contest that they are owned by their human, and would not seriously consider leaving – even if they were badly treated.

All this knowledge is important to ad agencies because in advertising they can "talk to" owners in a sympathetic way; demonstrating that they really understand pet ownership. Without such insights it would be impossible to project the brand of pet food being advertised as right for the owner, and pet too.

Chapter 13

Hong Kong and China, 1993–1995

After nine years of living out of suitcases, I longed for a return to a little more domestic stability, and looked for a job where my experience of both established and fledgling markets would be appreciated. My global role had been exciting and had given me a chance to see the world at someone else's expense, but enough was enough.

Then I was offered the chance to open up the biggest emerging market of all – China – whilst living in the comfort of one of the most exciting developed markets in the world, Hong Kong. Accepting this post was a 'no brainer': it would probably be the last move in my advertising career. Agency life is for the young and I was knocking on forty-six, after all!

Nevertheless, my new posting didn't start well. Landing at Hong Kong's old Kai Tak airport was an interesting experience at the best of times. If the pilot decided to approach the runway from the west, the plane would descend between high-rise apartment blocks, and to the inexperienced passenger, a crash into one of them seemed inevitable. This effect was magnified by the fact that Hong Kong residents dry their washing on long poles stuck out of apartment block windows. It seemed almost certain the plane would be strewn with clothing once it had (safely?) landed.

If the final approach was from the east, over Hong Kong Bay, passengers could be forgiven for thinking they would be swimming the last few yards, because the single narrow runway extending out into the bay couldn't be seen from the passenger windows on each side of the fuselage, so the plane would appear to be descending ever lower towards an inevitable crash into the sea.

On the day in question, matters were made much worse because we were landing during a typhoon. The captain had warned he might have to divert to a mainland Chinese airport, but then he announced he was going to "attempt a landing".

His words and rather strained tone did not improve the palpable fear most passengers felt, and my neighbour began praying audibly. My inaudible thought was: "Don't 'attempt a landing' *just get this f*****g crate down, captain.*"

Fortunately, he complied with my instruction. It was a bumpy landing, but we got there in one piece.

Others were not so lucky. Soon after our arrival, an Air China plane missed the runway and skidded sideways into Hong Kong Bay. I was amused that, having got the passengers to safety, the airline's next priority was to paint out its name and logo on the partly submerged fuselage, presumably to minimise the damage to the company's reputation. I was also amused when it was announced that all of the plane's passengers had disembarked safely but had each been given a large dose of antibiotics, seeing that the water in Hong Kong Bay was not exactly of drinkable quality.

My stay in Hong Kong was at a fascinating time, a couple of years before China was to take back the territory from the UK. Most of the locals I spoke to felt proud that their ethnic cousins would be taking over from their European colonial masters. Who would prefer to be ruled by a foreign colonial queen who lived thousands of miles away and seldom visited?

However, the UK had brought great prosperity and democracy to Hong Kong and had provided a stable political and business environment for all, under a transparent rule of law. Would their new masters in Beijing really maintain all that? Nowhere on earth could be said to be more capitalist than Hong Kong, while at the time, few countries could have claimed to be more communist than China. Could the citizens of Hong Kong trust China, seeing that many of them had fled the mainland for the freedoms of the colony in the previous few decades?

Either way, the takeover by China seemed inevitable. Interestingly, from a purely legal point of view, Britain could have retained the most important parts of the colony. While the New Territories were only leased to the UK and would have to be returned once the lease expired, most people did not realise that Hong Kong Island, and the ribbon of mainland immediately adjacent to it (Kowloon), had been ceded to Britain "in perpetuity". Nevertheless, retaining a small island thousands of miles away from the UK was obviously not practical for the government in London – an island that would be dominated by the landmass of China; a nation that could take Hong Kong back by force any time it wished by simply walking across the border.

When I arrived the handover was still years away, and most Chinese businesspeople gave the impression they were quite relaxed about it, but over a few beers the fears and uncertainties would surface. China had promised fifty years without significant change to the rule of law in its new acquisition, but already there was a general scramble to move personal investments (and sometimes whole families) overseas "just in case".

Getting a visa to enter China was a bit of a pain, but, as with Russia some years before, I was pleasantly surprised not to find armed police at every corner. Once past the formalities of immigration, the place felt relaxed and the people very friendly. Outside the major cities I soon got used to small children running up to touch me – presumably to make sure the strange looking European was real and solid, just like them.

I first entered China via the Kowloon–Canton Railway, which runs from Hong Kong to Guangzhou. The journey is perhaps the best way to get an introduction to China because of the very different views presented to a first-time traveller.

After crossing the border, the line runs through Shenzhen, a city designated in 1979 as China's first Special Economic Zone. This produced a frenzy of investment and the building of factories, offices, and accommodation for the workers. Pre-1979 it had had a population of thirty thousand, but by the time I left it had grown to an estimated ten million and been described by the UN as the world's fastest-growing city. Its high-rise buildings and bustling life made it look very much like an offshoot of Hong Kong, which essentially it was. Thereafter, the train passes through a rural landscape of rice fields and grazing water buffalo – a stark contrast indeed.

I inherited three fledgling offices in China; one in Beijing with six staff, one in Shanghai (one member of staff), and a third in Guangzhou (no staff as yet). They couldn't have been more different. Politically China is one country, but it hasn't really been a single entity for most of its history. The differences between the various regions are still very marked, though they are nominally unified now by a common language: Mandarin.

Guangzhou (or Canton, as many expats still called it) is geographically the closest long-established major Chinese city to Hong Kong and Macao, and is also the closest culturally to these two foreign colonies. During the last few centuries, the Chinese who set up settlements throughout South East Asia and owned laundries and restaurants across Europe and the Americas came largely from this province.

They were, and remain, the most adventurous and entrepreneurial citizens. In 1993, private enterprise was all but illegal in China, but a stroll through the side streets of Guangzhou required one to weave through family-owned food and commodity stalls, bespoke tailors, and all manner of other enterprises. The place hummed with commercial life based on these small family companies, while boasting very few of the high-rise blocks or other impressive buildings that can be seen in Shanghai and Beijing.

Shanghai couldn't have been more different. The skyline was filled with skyscraper offices and flats owned by foreign investors or government-run companies. There were few rich Chinese at this time, although the effects of a fast-growing middle class were beginning to be felt. The city was the home of big business rather than small family traders, and was proud to have been China's gateway to the world for centuries.

The Shanghainese consider themselves rather superior to the Chinese from other provinces. Shanghai always was a very cosmopolitan city, housing the head offices of foreign banks and other large businesses. Locals told me it was the epicentre of Chinese culture and art, while another boast was that 70% of all hairdressers and beauty parlours in the whole country were to be found there.

Our office had only one employee, a charming but rather quietly spoken woman. I later learned she lived alone because her parents – a doctor and a factory manageress – had been "re-educated" during the reign of Mao's wife by being sent to the country to "learn from the peasants about the true meaning of communism". They were picked up one night by plain-clothes police and never heard from again, the fate of so many "middle-class traitors". To survive, my employee was told to denounce them. Exactly what she had said and done I couldn't really ask, but the whole event had clearly left terrible mental scars.

My third office, in Beijing, was different again. While Shanghai could be said to be the centre of business, Beijing was the centre of bureaucracy and government, giving it a different sense of superiority. After all, it was the country's capital! It struck me that the two cities in many ways paralleled the differences between New York and Washington.

In Beijing I had a first-hand encounter with the infamous One Child Policy. With unsustainable annual population growth before the policy was introduced, and with the majority of the population being rural and poor, the government decided to act decisively. It decreed that no couple could have more than one child. In cities like Beijing the policy was rigorously enforced with threats of forced abortions. Lai Wah, my secretary, fell pregnant soon after I set up the office. She had had her pregnancy confirmed and a scan showed she was expecting a healthy girl.

In most societies this would be welcome news indeed, but having a son and heir is of prime importance throughout Asia. If she had had a daughter, the One Child Policy would mean Lai Wah would never have a chance to have a son. She lived with her husband and parents-in-law, all three of whom were pressuring her to have an abortion so the couple could try again for a son. She sought my advice, but this was one decision I could not become involved in.

Similar decisions were being made throughout China. The sum of the psychological distress caused is incalculable. The stupidity of it all was that the government did not need market research or a crystal ball to work out the effects on the population – that was obvious from the start. Population growth was cut, but China now has an ageing population that will hamper its economic future in the same way that mature markets such as Europe and Japan are suffering from an ageing workforce, with insufficient young graduates to join it.

China's early export success was based on a young, educated, hard-working and low-paid workforce. Increasingly these workers are now older, fewer, and demanding higher wages, with the result that countries such as Vietnam can undercut their bigger neighbour.

Another by-product of the One Child Policy was the growth of 'The Little Emperor Syndrome'. Family units typically comprised a boy, his parents, and his grandparents. The boy was spoiled rotten by his elders, who he could blackmail into giving him still more for good school results.

One further result has been the current wide gender disparity between those in their teens and twenties. Literally millions of young Chinese men will never marry unless they can find women from overseas, because of the slaughter of so many female foetuses.

Lai Wah decided to keep her daughter, but her decision led to her divorce. I increased her salary as far as I could without creating waves with the rest of the Beijing staff, and the two of us went shopping for nursery items before her successful delivery of a baby girl. Her ex-husband, who re-married, now has that all-important son.

China presented some fascinating problems to Western advertisers. For instance, we needed to make a TV commercial to promote the launch of a brand of food supplement to be taken by pregnant mothers in order to provide the foetus with all the nutrients it would require before birth. Not only was this a new product, it was a revolutionary idea.

It seems pregnant women in China had not considered the concept of feeding a foetus before, and if they had they would have had no idea which nutrients might be important. Young mothers-to-be in the West could get guidance from articles in the women's press, from ante-natal classes, or maybe from their mother or GP, but in this case there was no one to seek guidance from, aside from the traditional herbalists.

Our TV commercial featured an animated foetus in a womb who spoke to his mother by talking directly at the camera about his important nutritional needs, and how they could be easily and affordably met by buying this new imported supplement. At the beginning of the film, the foetus tugged on his umbilical cord to attract his mother's attention, then explained about the new product he wanted her to buy. Research later suggested that – once they had got over the initial shock of being spoken to by an unborn child – the target audience was amused and convinced by the message. The test market in Guangdong Province proved highly successful, and was supported by mailings to doctors and PR in publications we felt young women might read.

You are never too old to learn – as I was reminded when I helped my new client Budweiser launch its imported American beer at the Tsingtao Beer Festival. We unpacked the crates of bottles, glasses, T-shirts, and various other promotional materials and prepared for our first customers. Tired from our efforts and surrounded by beer, I opened two bottles, one for the client and one for myself. It was then I realised that the bottles contained more than the glasses could hold. Pointing out this error to the client, I suggested someone should be reprimanded for making such a basic mistake as packing the wrong glasses.

Not so, it seemed. Apparently the glasses used were intentionally too small, because that forced the bar staff to pass to the customer not only the glass (which had the Budweiser name and logo prominently printed on it), but the only partly empty bottle, which was also clearly branded. This would effectively provide free advertising once it was left on the bar or table, so other customers would know which brand was being consumed. True enough, once the beer festival was underway, only Budweiser bottles were visible in any quantity around the bars and tables. (These marketing people are *so* sneaky!)

The Chinese approach to business was very different to that which I had come to expect elsewhere. At the same beer festival, a senior director from one of the country's largest brands, Tsingtao Beer, asked me what I thought about launching his beer in Europe. I told him I felt confident there would be great interest in tasting the first "communist" beer. Correctly advertised, it might be possible to sell it at a significant premium over European brands. Furthermore, Chinese meals had become the most popular restaurant and take-away food in England, so the distribution of Tsingtao through Chinese eateries would generate significant extra volume for both the beer company and the restaurants.

He asked how much I thought would be needed to advertise the brand for a launch in the UK. He said he could afford to set aside £1 per case sold, to go towards marketing costs. I argued this was not the way to set budgets, because it suggested that sales create advertising, when logically it was advertising that created sales. I recommended he should start by investing in advertising, in order to enjoy future profits through future sales.

He laughed, threw up his hands and walked away. "Investing in future sales" was not the Chinese way at all it seemed.

In contrast, it was certainly how the insightful few Western companies did business in China. An American pet food advertiser decided to invest heavily in its launch of canned and dry pet food in the country.

Initially, this struck me as brave (if not crazy) in a land noted more for eating dogs than feeding them, particularly as the client was talking of a marketing budget far larger than the company would be likely to earn in gross sales - in the first few years at least. Owning pets in China was also not that common either. In fact, owning dogs was illegal in some cities. Plus, there was only a small middle class likely to want (or be able to afford) to feed their dog this premium imported pet food - if they had a dog in the first place.

How wrong I was. In the next few years, a middle class with significant disposable income became more and more apparent, as did the ownership of expensive imported pedigree dogs, which became a status symbol. China was changing *fast*, and the client proved to be astute in establishing its brands before any competitor had decided the country was worth the candle.

While most of my time was spent in China, the advertising campaign I most remember was developed in Hong Kong for local use there. On a 'pro bono' basis, we handled a charity that flew a specially adapted aeroplane to various airports in China to offer blind and partially sighted children free eye operations. It was seeking donations to maintain its busy schedule.

We designed a small press campaign for the charity. With a tiny budget, the black-and-white ad was quite small, so it had to be very impactful to be seen, read, and acted upon. It simply featured an illustration of an old TV set, under which were the words:

"To over 6,000,000 Chinese children, this is a radio."

The campaign won the top Hong Kong advertising industry award that year, and through the donations it generated saved the sight of thousands of Chinese children.

Such campaigns, designed for non-profit-making organisations, make me feel proud of my industry. Some of the very best creativity is used for these ads rather than being reserved for major clients, upon whom an agency's profitability depends.

Budgets for such campaigns are always small, so stand-out ads are particularly necessary. A TV campaign by a competitor in the region for a "Don't drink and drive" campaign is a wonderful example.

The "one shot" commercial showed an evening street scene as viewed through a car's windscreen from the driving seat of a car. After perhaps five seconds, an empty beer glass is placed on the dashboard in front of the driver. Forced to look through the glass to see the street, the driver's view becomes a little distorted. A few seconds later a second empty glass is placed behind the first one, making the driver's view further distorted. Finally, a third glass is placed on the dashboard making the driver's view of his surroundings virtually impossible. There is the sound of emergency breaking, a loud bang, and the screen goes black.

A simple message pops onto the screen to make the point (should it be necessary) that one drink effects the ability to drive and causes many accidents. Further drinks are even more likely to lead to accidents and can be lethal. The short campaign was found to be emotionally disturbing (in a positive sense) and caused a major stir.

If only all campaigns worked this well!

Chapter 14

To Travel No More

As I have said to friends many times, advertising is a 'sport' for the young, and I had begun to feel less than 100% comfortable in the testosterone-charged atmosphere I sensed around me in the various offices I visited. The incessant travel, 'revitalising' beers and almost nightly client dinners were taking their toll. I was unfit, overweight, and tired, yet I was still two years short of my fiftieth birthday.

No one retires at forty-eight, do they?

Why not? I owned a nice apartment in London, which had leapt in value over the last two decades. I had a modest portfolio of shares, and my various pensions should be enough to support me once I started to draw on them when I had hit fifty-five. I was very fond of South East and East Asia and its way of life, but I was British and I felt sure I would settle back into life "at home" one day.

What to do?

Once again, Fate largely made my decision for me. During a working trip to western China, I picked up a nasty dose of a potentially fatal condition called Necrotising Fasciitis.

I was doing a dealership presentation on a new car launch in Sichuan province in the far west of the country. As I stood on the stage, a throbbing ache in my left leg that had bothered me all morning just wouldn't go away. During questions, I found it hard to concentrate as the pain increased.

Back in my hotel room, I could see that my left foot and lower leg had turned black! I flew back to Beijing as soon as I could, where luckily my hotel contacted the Sino-German Clinic. I was seen by a Dutch doctor who was in China on a protracted period of leave from Amsterdam University Hospital to be with her husband, a Shell senior manager based in China. While the condition is rare, she recognised the symptoms, flooded my body with antibiotics, and immediately put me on a plane to Hong Kong.

Tucked up in bed in a Hong Kong hospital, what little reassurance I'd been given in Beijing about my medical future was dissipated by a consultant who attended me with a group of young doctors in tow.

"As you can see, the black swelling has reached just above the patient's knee. I'll mark the limit of it by drawing around the leg with this magic marker. We'll come back in two hours, and if the discoloration moves above the line, we'll amputate."

Nothing is more dehumanising than having your condition discussed as though you weren't there. Not only that, but it would seem I wasn't going to be given any say in the matter of potentially losing my leg!

I spent the next two hours desperately willing the swelling to recede. The consultant returned punctually after two hours, his 'tail' of white-coated medical students still trailing behind him.

"Nothing seems to have happened to the swelling. We'll give it another two hours."

They say 'time flies when you're enjoying yourself', but when you have just two hours to save your leg from the scalpel, time really does seem to take wings. Ultimately, my leg – and the rest of me – survived, but my experience made up my mind.

I was going home.

My last three months in Hong Kong and China were chaotic. First I had to "break in" my successor. Philip was bright and keen, but had hardly left his native New York in his fifteen-year career, so not only was he experiencing Asia for the first time, it was his first time working outside New York State too.

His wife and four-year-old daughter would also have a lot to adjust to in this foreign environment, especially with Philip out of the house frequently, visiting his various offices. Imagine running the oldest Western advertising agency in China (then only three years old) under such circumstances – particularly if you speak no Mandarin (as I didn't either). Not to mention running the office in Hong Kong with its 180 staff as well, even if most of them spoke a "sensible" language.

I had packing to be done, and friends and clients alike to say goodbye to. But most importantly, I had to decide what I wanted to do next. Would I fly straight home to London or, since I was on the other side of the world, take my time by returning in a series of short hops? The bulk of my belongings could be sent on ahead. After all, there were still many countries I hadn't visited, and many others I had enjoyed and would like to see again without all the limitations of visiting them on business. I was in no particular hurry anyway.

My decision-making process reminded me of the son of my second boss back in London many years earlier. Nigel was a bright, outward-going teenager who had done well at public school and had won himself a place at Oxford to read Law. However, like so many in his position, he decided to take a sabbatical year before settling down to five years of intensive study. He planned to work his way gradually around the world to Australia, taking any work he could find along the way to help pay for his travels.

By month five he'd arrived in Thailand – and there he stayed longer than he'd expected, in fact at least the next twenty years. He travelled to the island of Koh Phi Phi and fell in love with it and its laid-back way of life, while simultaneously falling in love with a Thai girl. They lived in a basic, one-room, hut-like house just off the main beach. When not relaxing or fishing, he worked for a local travel agent taking tourists to the various places of interest on the island during the day, and then on to the bars, restaurants, and massage parlours in the evening. It must have been hell!

His parents had been heart broken, but I felt jealous of his decision making. Had he been wrong to "throw away his life" and a promising career in the law, or was he correct to live a life of his own choosing in a beautiful setting, doing what he really wanted to do with the woman he loved?

In contrast, I had let Fate move my career from job to job. It was true that Nigel might find old age in Thailand (with no National Health Service or state pension) harder than in England, but after perhaps fifty years of working in paradise as a career, maybe it would have been all worthwhile.

Having given back the keys to my flat, I spent the last two weeks in Hong Kong in the Mandarin Hotel for my final farewells and to plan my "escape" from advertising. During my stay I came to know the Resident Manager, and the two of us spent many evenings together in one bar or another once he was off duty.

One evening we were sipping our beers watching an old British comedy programme - the episode of *Fawlty Towers* where the owner, Basil, is nervously showing a hotel inspector around his premises, only to learn that a guest had died in one of the bedrooms.

A panicking Basil makes his excuses, and eventually the corpse, covered in used sheets, is wheeled out past the inspector in a wicker laundry basket. After the show had finished, I commented on how funny my friend had evidently found the episode.

"You don't understand," he said. "That sort of thing really happens! If you ever open a hotel, the first thing you should do is find an 'understanding' doctor. That way, if a guest dies you can call the doctor in so he can say that the patient doesn't look at all well and should go to hospital, just in case. If the guest is found to be dead on arrival at the hospital, that becomes their problem. A death in one of our rooms means blocking off the room, calling a doctor, then the police so they can decide there was no foul play, holding the room until the body is removed, fumigating it, etc.,

etc. It's a nightmare, it's bad for business and it's very upsetting for the staff.

"I remember," he continued, "in a previous posting of mine in Hong Kong, an American tourist, part of a tour group, was found dead when his room service breakfast was delivered. By this time rigor mortis had set in and he wasn't a pretty sight. The doctor was called. He duly decided that the man wasn't looking at all well and that an ambulance should be called. But it was important to get the guest out of the room before the ambulance arrived so there was no evidence of where he had died.

"So we got a wheelchair to take him to the back door via the staff lift. Getting his stiffened limbs into the wheelchair took some time – we had to nearly break his legs to make them bend so he would sit 'comfortably' with a blanket over his knees. As we headed for the staff lift, an old lady from his tour group saw us and asked if Mr Carnegie was alright. I explained that he wasn't feeling 100%, so he was going to hospital… just to be on the safe side."

Eventually I decided I would make a short trip to Vietnam (which I had never visited before), then travel on to see all my friends in Singapore, before going up to Bangkok for similar goodbyes, then New Delhi, Dubai, and home. But that is not quite how things worked out.

Unfortunately my first stop, Vietnam, proved a bit of a disappointment. Having been spoiled by Oriental cuisine in many South East and East Asian countries, I found Viet cuisine uninspiring. Saigon had little I found inspiring either. I soon had had enough of the admittedly very impressive classical French architecture, and had declined the offer of crawling through some tunnels dug by the Vietcong during their "little disagreement" with the Americans. The beaches nearby were good, but what country in the region that has a coastline doesn't have great beaches?

I probably lacked a good guide. There must have been more I could have enjoyed, but after five days I headed back to the airport.

However, there was one quirk about the country I will always remember, though I'm sure I will disappoint many by having this as my defining memory of Vietnam.

On my first morning, a bell boy handed me a small leaflet as I headed towards the main doors of my hotel to go exploring. With it in my hand, I stepped out into the street and was faced with a noisy, fume-ridden main road with perhaps seven or eight lanes of traffic, all moving in the same direction.

Although the traffic was heavy, cars and lorries were moving at a surprising pace, while motorbikes weaved between them at an even faster pace. It seemed a miracle that there were not repeated accidents right there in front of me. I could see no footbridge, zebra crossing, traffic lights, underpass, or other visible way for pedestrians to cross.

Stumped for a moment, I looked at the leaflet in my hand while waiting for inspiration. Finding the page that was in English, I began reading.

WARNING

We would like you to enjoy your stay in our city, but would wish to advise you, for your safety, regarding the best way to cross the avenue outside our hotel, and all other major roads you may come across in our beautiful city. To traverse safely, please always do the following:

- **Decide where you want to cross.**
- **Wait until you see a small gap in the traffic in the lane nearest to your pavement.**
- **Take a single step forward. Do not be concerned about approaching vehicles – they will see you, brake, or swerve to avoid you.**
- **Take further steps forward at a slow steady pace. *Do not* speed up or slow down for any reason as this will confuse vehicles trying to avoid you.**

- *Do not change direction*, and most important of all, *do not try to turn back*. This would be most dangerous.

Have a wonderful and safe stay in our great city.

My next destination, Singapore, has become a tourist's delight, to be recommended to all. To me it feels almost like home. Changi airport is undoubtedly the best in the world. How many do you know with cinemas and top-rated restaurants, plus a rooftop swimming pool and jacuzzi?

I jumped into a taxi – they all have meters that actually work, which is close to unique in Asia – and told the driver my destination.

"Why you want Racecourse Road, boss?"

"Because I really fancy a fish-head curry at the Banana Leaf."

"Oh, you know Singapore food?"

"Yes, I lived here many years ago."

"You must try Hainanese Chicken Rice at Mount Faber, boss."

"No, the rice is better at the Ministry of Social Affairs staff canteen."

"Really? I not know that one. Maybe I try, lah."

The rest of the journey was spent exchanging restaurant tips. I was chuffed to be able to give as good as I got about the best places to eat in the city the driver had lived in all his life.

That evening was spent at a restaurant on the beach at the East Coast Parkway with a dozen or so of my former staff, who were by now my firm friends. We had chilli crab, sea bass steamed in soy sauce and *sotong* (small deep-fried squid), all washed down with Tiger beer of course. Gourmet heaven!

After a calorie-filled week, I left for Bangkok.

Within a few hours of touching down at the new Bangkok airport, I was relaxing on a lounger by the pool at my old haunt, the Oriental Hotel, cradling a very cold Singha Beer. My neighbour on the next lounger, was similarly relaxing with a beer in his hand. He leaned over and said, "This is Paradise, isn't it?"

For some reason I didn't just smile an acknowledgement, but considered his statement in some detail. My situation relaxing by the pool was highly enjoyable, but I would not ever have described Bangkok as "Paradise". Surely Paradise has a degree of order, quiet peacefulness, and purity – words I had never heard used to describe Bangkok. But for all its failings, I felt very happy to be back. And the Oriental has been repeatedly voted the best hotel in the world, so maybe I wasn't too far from Paradise after all.

Sigh. Sip. Relax. Repeat.

I did nothing that day but eat, drink, and take life easy, but the next day I wanted to explore. Bangkok is a big and rapidly changing city in which I hadn't spent much time for many years, and I felt I would be wasting an opportunity if I didn't experience something new before flying home.

I discussed my goal with the concierge. Thai was my favourite cuisine, so would he recommend where I could get the *very best* Thai food? Somewhere Thais would know but to which tourists would not be taken?

He suggested an open-air restaurant to the north of the city if I didn't mind an hour's taxi ride. I didn't mind at all.

The place didn't look that special. I asked the English-speaking waitress to recommend dishes for me, something unusual I would remember for a long time. I had to ask because the menu was all in Thai, and I was hoping for a new experience anyway. She wondered if I would like seafood. I nodded and watched her go to the kitchen with my order.

A few minutes later, a simple charcoal barbecue was wheeled over - a large earthenware bowl partly filled with glowing coals. Then, a small cloth-covered table was carried over, which I correctly guessed held the raw food.

The chef arrived, a smiling, delightful young woman in a sarong. When she removed the cloth, I saw a lobster, crab, some prawns, and a white fish I didn't recognise. It was far too much for me to eat, though I managed to finish it all over a two-hour meal with no difficulty at all. The food was cooked to perfection, but the chef's secret was the blend of sauces, marinades, herbs, and spices, which made the whole meal so unforgettable. With the help of the waitress as translator, I learned as much as I could about the chef's culinary secrets... and about her as well.

She had been working in Bangkok for two years, but originally came from a small village on the Thai–Cambodian border. Like so many people working in Bangkok, she tried hard to send money home each month. Rural salaries were only just adequate during years when the rice harvest was good, but in bad years her monthly financial assistance was a real lifeline for her mother, father, and brother, all of whom had a rather hand-to-mouth existence.

For the next three days, I returned to the same restaurant for lunch and made sure the same charming, and really quite beautiful, chef looked after me. I was fascinated by her descriptions of life in her home village. She even taught me a few swear words in Khmer, just for a laugh. It was a shame we needed a translator, but the waitress seemed to enjoy bridging the linguistic gap between two people who clearly got on so well.

In truth, I was a little disappointed when the time came to fly home to Heathrow.

Chapter 15

Paradise

I settled into daily life in London and it was good to be back, but even so, I found I missed Thailand.

I flew back four months later and returned to my favourite restaurant and my favourite chef. I was surprised and thrilled to find that, while I'd been away, she'd started to learn English.

All Thais seem to have a nickname, and hers was Lek, which means 'Tiny' – which hardly described my 5 foot 7 inch new friend. She gave me the nickname 'Chang Khou', meaning 'white elephant' in Khmer. I wasn't too sure about it, but it was bestowed with a giggle and a kiss on the cheek.

I travelled to Bangkok three times a year for the next three years. It became obvious to both Lek and I that we enjoyed spending time together. I wanted to be with her and was keen to see the village she spoke so much about, plus her family as well. I had begun learning Thai in London, while her English was becoming ever more fluent, so increasingly we managed to communicate more fully, without help, in one language or the other.

Lek was so excited as we drove the four hundred kilometres to her village near Prasat Muang Tam in Buriram Province. She explained that Buriram meant "City of Happiness" in Khmer, which sounded like a good omen to me. The main road out of Bangkok was in decent condition, but the further we travelled the slower the taxi was forced to go in order to navigate potholes and other obstructions. Perhaps thirty kilometres from the village we began travelling on simple, unmade dirt tracks, which must have been less than fun in the monsoon season.

When we pulled up, the family came out of the house to greet us and immediately made me feel welcome. Their home was a single-room wooden structure; little more than a large garden shed really – except that it was two foot off the ground on low stilts. It really did have only one room: no kitchen, bathroom, storeroom, or loo. One room to eat in (if it rained), and the same room to sit in and sleep in. No electricity. All food cooked on an open fire outside. Illumination by candlelight or paraffin lamp.

People always ask how I managed with no bathroom. Washing was accomplished wearing swimming trunks and ladling water out of a rainwater butt over my head. It couldn't have been more basic, but it kept me clean. (OK, cleanish.) Other necessary bodily functions were accomplished in a similar rudimentary fashion a little further away.

I noticed that under the house were three concrete beams that seemed to serve no useful purpose. Lek explained that when she sent money home, her father would save as much as he could until he could afford to order another beam. The objective was to replace the current wooden "shed" with a sturdier structure when enough beams had been collected.

During my second visit to the village, I was very proud to see the new concrete-framed home I had been able to buy for them, constructed close to the old one. It was a simple A-frame structure that would last much longer than the wooden version next door. And it had electricity connected too, so no more candles after dusk. It cost all of £7,000.

I would happily have spent more on these wonderful people, but Lek did not want me to be seen as some ugly, rich, boastful foreigner. A "palace" among the other huts in the village would have made everyone feel uncomfortable. As it was, even the new house was beyond the family's dreams.

Soon after that, Lek left her job in Bangkok and spent all her time with her family. I visited three or four times a year. I was really happy in her company and my feelings for her continued to grow. However, spending so much time in aeroplanes and even more time alone in London was not how I wanted my life to continue. It was not ideal for Lek either, who began to feel bored when I wasn't around; the village could hardly be described as full of exciting things to do, particularly for someone unemployed, as she had become with my financial support.

So we decided to get married.

But before that, we designed and built a home for ourselves. Lek wanted to run a bar, which would be the social focus for the eight hundred people of the village and those beyond, and would keep her busy (though certainly not very rich) when I was away. My focus was the accommodation on the first floor above the bar, because I wanted a bit more comfort for my old age than a single-roomed wooden dwelling on stilts could provide.

In just eighteen months, the construction of our new home and business was finished and we were able to move in. The bar offered drinks and freshly cooked snacks, plus two pool tables, a dartboard, a big colour TV and music. Villagers travelled some distance to enjoy an evening in such 'luxury'. Upstairs were two bedrooms, a kitchen/dining area, lounge, bathroom, lavatory, and office.

Once all the legal paperwork making Lek the owner had been completed, (I remembered what had happened to Barry and Yuwadi), we got married in the grounds of the ancient Khmer temple in Prasat Muang Tam. It was all very romantic. I had been dodging marriage and commitment all my adult life, but I couldn't have been happier to be "trapped" by Lek. And I've gained a family, even if I can only have the simplest of conversations with its members. Strange though it might sound, my old life and my new one blended together seamlessly.

I still spend time in my London flat, frequently accompanied by my new wife. I still lecture to young graduates at a London advertising agency about the mysteries of international advertising and marketing, and when in Thailand I'm a guest lecturer at Buriram Rajabhat University.

How will my life eventually end up? I really have no idea. I'll leave that to 'He who is way, way above my pay grade'. He has done a pretty good job of making my life's decisions for me so far.